CW00554024

LINCOLN CORPORATION TRA

BY

CYRIL COOKE

This edition published in 2006 by:-
Firs Publishing
Canwick, Lincoln

ISBN 0-9546074-4-9

© Cyril Cooke

Typeset By:-
Joyce Jefford and Pelican Trust Ltd

Printed By:-
Pelican Trust Ltd, Allenby Industrial Estate, Lincoln

CONTENTS

FOREWORD

I was born in Lincoln in 1950 and lived in various parts of the City until moving with my family to the Burton Road area in 1954.

My schooldays began at Mount Street Infants School and continued at Westgate Junior School and Rosemary Secondary Modern, where I became interested in woodwork and metalwork. Finally I attended the Lincoln Technical College for four years on both a pre-apprenticeship craft course and latterly on day-release courses.

I first became fascinated by buses as a young boy travelling with my mother into town on the Bristol K type buses of the Lincolnshire Road Car fleet, from our home at Hampden Square off Skellingthorpe Road. I also watched with interest when the buses arrived at Westgate School each day to take children home to the Ermine Estate. By the time I was 13 years of age I knew all the fleet numbers and registrations of all the buses in the Lincoln Corporation fleet. The many different styles of coachwork inspired me to become an apprentice coachbuilder with the local firm of Charles Warner in 1966.

In 1965 I joined the Lincolnshire Vintage Vehicle Society and there, from 1966 to 1970, I was engaged in rebuilding the bodywork of a dilapidated Leyland Titan double decker bus that was originally in the Bolton Corporation Transport fleet from 1929 to 1936. Putting aside my trade for a while I went on the road as one of the last conductors on the Lincoln Corporation buses in February 1978, became a crew driver and then a one-man operator in August that year. The first bus I drove in service after acquiring my public service vehicle licence was Leyland Panther No 41, of which I am now the proud owner.

Another period in the woodwork trade spanned 10 years, including 5 years for the Dean and Chapter of Lincoln Cathedral, where I was charge hand in the joiners' workshop. Today I work as a driver once again, for Lincoln's largest independent coach company, P C Coaches of Lincoln.

It was as long ago as 1968 when the idea for this book was first mentioned in conversation with the late Mr Vincent Le Tall, founder member of the LVVS. Looking at photographs of buses and also discussing progress on the Leyland Titan restoration project in his office at Higgs Tobacconists one Saturday morning, he suggested I should write the history of our Lincoln buses. That suggestion remained in my mind for many years and eventually led me to gather the facts and items of interest about the company.

In 1982 I had the pleasure of meeting, for the first time, Mr William Kirk, Lincoln's last surviving tramway motorman. I very much appreciated all his help and interest and I pay tribute to him in two of the photograph captions.

There has been a vast amount of photographs to choose from, and I am now proud to present the full history of Lincoln Corporation Transport. The book is a tribute to all the many people employed by LCT over the years who daily kept the vehicles running. All the trams and buses served the City well, and it is difficult to have one favourite vehicle or favourite type. Throughout, the book has been carefully researched and all the dates quoted are as accurate as possible. It should appeal to both enthusiasts and all the many people who may take only a passing interest in buses and the City.

I would like to thank all the people who have helped with information and the reproduction of the photographs. Care has been taken to trace copyright holders of all the photographs. My apologies are tendered if any infringement has occurred.

CYRIL COOKE

ACKNOWLEDGEMENTS

Tom Bunnage	LCT Conductor
Paul Cooke	Photographer
Geoff Espin	T & G Workers Union
The late Geoffrey Fletcher	LCT Driver
The late Tom Freeman	LCT Inspector
Peter Grey	Photographer
Maurice Hodson	Archivist
Ray Hooley	Ruston & Hornsby
Joyce Jefford	Typist
Nigel Kirk	Photographer
Russell Kirk	Photographer
The late William Kirk	LCT Motorman/Driver
The late F V LeTall	LVVS Founder Member
Lincoln Central Library	
Lincolnshire Echo	
LVVS Archive Collection	
Roy Marshall	Photographer
The late John Middleton	Photographer
Arnold Richardson	Photobus Collection
Don Teesdale	LVVS Trustee
The late Fred White	LCT Workshop Superintendent

INTRODUCTION

The origin of the charming City of Lincoln, with its beautiful Cathedral standing high on the limestone plateau, can be traced back many thousands of years.

The Bronze and Iron Age people began their settlement by the pool and along the banks of the river Witham. They gave it the name Lindon. In Celtic the first part of the name Llyn, means pool. When the Romans came in AD 48 they built a timber fortress, establishing a garrison on the hilltop by about AD 60. They Latinised the name Lindon to Lindum. By AD 96 the legions had moved on to York and Chester and the fortress became a chartered town and centre for veteran Legionary soldiers. The Emperor Domitian, recognised the centre's great strength and importance and confirmed it with the status of Colonia. Hence it became Lindum Colonia from which the present name Lincoln, is directly derived.

Lindum Colonia became a thriving commercial centre. Agriculture and the wool trade were the main industries of the surrounding countryside. There were also many pottery kilns distributing their wares from the Lindum area.

There was a growth in prosperity within the Colonia, and the walls, which by this time were stone, were extended and many magnificent new buildings were erected within.

A prosperous suburb developed outside the walls and beyond the river Witham from about AD 250.

Centuries later, new wealth came due to the Industrial Revolution and canal improvements, followed by the arrival of the railways and Lincoln's many heavy engineering foundries.

It was because of Lincoln's unusual geological division into uphill and downhill, with steep narrow streets linking the two halves, that it was late in getting public street transport when compared to other towns and cities.

Interest was shown by the Sheffield and Manchester Railway in 1859 in operating a short tramway from Gas Street (near the old gas works, Carholme Road) and along the south bank of the pool. Little is known about this plan but bearing in mind the large expanse of land south of the pool was the Holmes Common until the arrival of the railway, perhaps the intention was to take visitors to the City from the railway station along the bank of the pool. It is known there were complications associated with this route and turntables would have to have been installed so the system was not constructed.

The growth in traffic on the railways coupled with the expansion in engineering had increased Lincoln's population. Victorian housing development was largely concentrated to the south and east of the City centre. The majority were back-to-back terraces.

By 1880 housing had spread south down the High Street as far as Bracebridge village.

That year Messrs Jackson and Son established a service running three horse drawn omnibuses between the City centre and Bracebridge, a distance of nearly two miles. There was a flat fare of two old pennies (2d).

Plans were deposited by another company, "Lincoln Tramways" to obtain permission by Act of Parliament to construct a 3ft 6ins gauge tramway along the same route.

An Act of Parliament was also sought by a third company "Lincolnshire Tramways" in the same year to construct a 3ft 6ins gauge tramway along the east side of Ermine Street, the old Roman carriage way from Brigg to Lincoln. On reaching Rasen Lane just north of the Cathedral, the line was to turn to run northwest along Burton Road as far as the junction with Yarborough Road. At that point a reversal was to have taken place for the descent of the Yarborough hillside (a gradient of 1 in 20). Both plans were approved by Parliament in 1881. The Lincoln Tramways company was authorised to construct the line from Bracebridge to the Stonebow Archway on the High Street. From there the track was to branch west along Guildhall Street, Newland, and Carholme Road almost as far as the Carholme race course, thus providing a connection with Lincolnshire Tramways, Brigg to Lincoln route. A second branch line from the High Street route was to have curved east beyond the Stonebow, running along Silver Street and Monks Road, terminating at the Arboretum. That would have given Lincoln Tramways three routes and about four miles of track. However, only the Bracebridge route was laid.

The service commenced operation in 1882 with two horse drawn cars running from the Gatehouse Hotel at Bracebridge to St Benedict's Church on Lincoln High Street. The fare was one old penny (1d) per stage and there were two stages. The competition soon led to the horse buses going out of business.

During 1884 some track was laid along Ermine Street forming the first part of the Lincoln-Brigg scheme but the line owned by Mr Joshua Bryant was never completed. It would have become the longest rural tramcar route in Great Britain. Plans for the electric tramways were published in 1899 in a report by the Corporation's Electricity Manager, Mr S Vesey Brown. He envisaged a network of electric tram routes from the High Street along Monks Road, Carholme Road, Yarborough Road, Burton Road and the High Street to Bracebridge with a possible takeover of the Lincoln Tramways. The City Council took up his proposals and in 1900 an Act of Parliament was obtained to construct these lines.

The Lincoln Motor Bus and Parcel Delivery Company began operation in 1900 with four large, eight seat Motor Cars. They worked a circular service from the Arboretum on Monks Road travelling via Silver Street, Mint Street, Newland, Carholme Road, Moor Street and then returning via West Parade, Corporation Street, Butchery Street (now re-named Clasketgate) and Monks Road.

Lengthy negotiations took place between the City Council and the Lincoln Tramways company regarding a takeover.

The Burton Road and Newport areas had become built up by 1900 and needed a transport link with the City Centre. If electric tramcars had been run up the Yarborough Road it would have involved a reversal of the cars at the top of the hill at its junction with Burton Road and this was deemed indirect. An alternative proposal was a branch along Carline Road, Drury Lane to Castle Square. The project was abandoned.

In 1904 the Lincoln Tramways was purchased by the Lincoln Corporation and the following year the Bracebridge route was electrified.

A scheme was produced by Mr R Lilly in 1909 to construct a Funicular railway up Steep Hill to Castle Square, a gradient of 1 in 5. His proposal was not accepted.

Motorbus trials were held by the Corporation in 1912/13 but due to the outbreak of World War I in 1914, it was not until 1920 that the first motorbuses were put into service.

Mr Richard Bray of St Catherine's Road converted a taxi into a small bus circa 1918/19. He ran two services into Lincoln. One from Bracebridge Heath through to the Bowling Green on Wragby Road. The second ran from Swanpool to the City. In 1920 he was forbidden by the Corporation to carry on operating these two routes.

Lincoln tramways ran a fleet of ten tramcars of three different types. Eight were one-horse saloons for general use and there were two toastracks for summer service. Two of the saloons were purchased second-hand from Gravesend in 1899. On light passenger loadings the horses worked three journeys before being rested, if loadings were heavy they worked two journeys. In bad weather two horses were yoked up to each car to maintain the timetable. This photograph was taken at the Bracebridge terminal outside the Gatehouse Hotel.

MAURICE HODSON COLLECTION

Horse tramcar No 3 passes the goods office of the Midland Railway on the last journey on 22 July 1905. The service ended with seven tramcars in the fleet and a total of twenty-two fine horses.

MAURICE HODSON COLLECTION

Work on the track was in progress when this photograph was taken circa 1905-1910. The state of the trenches indicates that maintenance work may have been being carried out to the surface contact system rather than the junction just being installed as new. This is the Cross O' Cliff Hill junction and the parking track can be seen on the left.

FROM THE LOCAL STUDIES COLLECTION, LINCOLN CENTRAL LIBRARY
BY COURTESY OF LINCOLNSHIRE COUNTY COUNCIL,
EDUCATION AND CULTURAL SERVICES DIRECTORATE

1904-1929

PART 1 CITY OF LINCOLN TRAMWAYS

In June 1904 the Lincoln Tramways Company was purchased by the Lincoln Corporation at the price of £10,488. The Corporation continued operating the horse tramcars until 22 July 1905. The last tram was worked by Mr George Pimp.

A temporary service was then operated with passengers being carried in wagonettes whilst the route was re-tracked and a stud contact electric power supply laid under the roadway.

This type of power pick up made by Griffiths Bedell was chosen by the Council after a great deal of debate on the subject of electrification.

The appearance of the City was considered and the City Fathers said that the installation of an overhead arrangement of wires fixed to serried ranks of standards would completely spoil the appearance of the High Street with its occasional sweeping curves and long vistas.

Lincoln was one of the first authorities to install the stud contact system.

Eight new double deck tramcars built by Brush of Loughborough were purchased. Six were open top and two were covered top. Electric tramway operation began on 23 November 1905 with Mr Pimp at the controls of the first car in service. The journey, just under two miles from Bracebridge to St Benedict's was scheduled to take fifteen minutes (five minutes less than the horses).

There were seventeen request stops along the route, which in places was only single track.

Loops at various places enabled the cars to pass and were at the least, long enough to accommodate three waiting cars if necessary and timing to pass at those places was important to avoid delays. The largest section of double track stretched from Cross O' Cliff to Portland Street. The other five loops were located at the Cornhill, between the Northern and Midland railway crossings, St Catherine's, Fairfax Street and the terminal loop at the Gatehouse Hotel in Bracebridge.

The route was converted to overhead electric supply in 1919 as a result of the stud contact system not being entirely successful. On many occasions crews had to push their cars to engage a live stud. As well as this, much work had to be done to keep the studs free from grit and dust. A wire brush was trailed at one end of each car for this purpose.

Three additional covered top, double deck tramcars were bought in 1919, built by Dick Kerr & Co mounted on English Electric trucks and they became Nos 9, 10, 11. They were delivered in workshop grey primer and they worked in service in that colour for a short time prior to receiving their pale green and cream livery. Two horse cars were purchased second-hand in 1918 from Great Grimsby Street Tramways Co and these were used as trailers at busy periods. Some modifications to the tramcars were carried out from time to time. This included fitting lower end vestibules, enclosed balconies and roofs. Each car had a sliding door at each end, on the partition bulkhead behind the motorman. The door in the forward direction of travel was closed and locked. The top deck balcony door was also locked so that all boarding and alighting was at the rear of the cars.

Longitudinal bench seats made of perforated plywood were fitted in the lower saloons whilst those on the top decks were made of wooden slats mounted on steel frames. These transverse seats had reversible backs for the direction of travel.

All the tramcars were painted in a beautiful standard livery of pale green, cream and black. The original layout was: lower deck panels were half pale green above half cream, curved lower ends pale green. Top deck side panels and balconies cream with a narrow green waistband. Window frames cream and roofs black. The fleet numbers affixed at each end were gold leaf shaded in red as also was the company title, City of Lincoln Tramways. The trucks were painted in red oxide.

The tramcars provided a very efficient service and to quote the late Mr Bertram Barnsdale, former tramcar motorman, later inspector and employed by the tramways since 1902: "sometimes as many as eighty or more passengers rode from the City centre to Gowts Bridge". When football matches were being played at Sincil Bank, passenger loadings were heavy so extra trams were on service. A parking track was used for these additional cars and this was located at the lower end of Cross O' Cliff Hill by the South Common The duplicate trams would park until the game was over then they were put into service to cope with the increased loadings.

During the 1914-18 war, conductresses were promoted to drive the cars as male drivers were in short supply. In the event of an air raid warning the current was cut off for ten seconds and then all cars returned to the depot until the all clear was given. On the High Street, railway signals were located at both the Great Northern and Midland railway crossings and motormen had to obey.

When cars were being worked in foggy weather conditions, fog staffs were used for safety. Before entering a single-track section a driver had to wait for a departing tram on that section to receive the staff. Once in possession of the staff, the driver could proceed in the knowledge that no other car was on that section.

The tramways were well patronized and made a profit but were seen as an outdated mode of transport by new Manager Mr Richard Hoggard who was appointed in October 1920. He suggested the way forward was expansion of motorbus operation as they could reach all parts of the City. To expand the tramway operation as outlined by Mr Vesey Brown in 1899 would have needed huge investment for track and points. The decline of the tramways was evident when the Council gave approval to Mr Hoggard in 1927 to order a batch of ten Leyland double-decked motorbuses. During 1928 and the early part of 1929 they worked the High Street routes alongside the trams.

The decision to abandon the tramway system was taken by the City Council in August 1928. On 4 March 1929 tramcar No 6 was driven on the last journey from the War Memorial to Bracebridge by Mr Charlie Hill. It was gaily decorated with flags and carried members of the City Council and the Transport Department. The latest motorbus No 34, was also decorated with flags for the occasion and it carried the members back to the City. From then onwards the Bracebridge route became bus Route 7 and ran from St Mary's Street to Bracebridge. The Doddington Road Route 4 was also re-routed via High Street and Newark Road to provide additional journeys.

Brush tramcar No 6 was the first electric car to be operated on the Bracebridge to Lincoln route in a pre-service trial on 23 October 1905. The trial run was to test both the tramcar and the efficiency of the Griffiths Bedell stud contact, power pick-up system. A lot of interest was shown by the general public in this new form of transport.

MAURICE HODSON COLLECTION

This second photograph of No 6 on the trial day also shows construction work being carried out on the former horse tram depot at Bracebridge. The façade had to be rebuilt to provide headroom for the new double deck cars.

MAURICE HODSON COLLECTION

Public service of the electric tramcars began four weeks later on 23 November 1905. This photograph taken in 1906 shows the High Street looking north towards the Cathedral. Tramcar No 1 has just departed from the St Benedict's terminal and is about to pass St Mary's church.

LVVS COLLECTION

The last two Brush tramcars supplied were built with upper deck bulkheads and top covers. Car No 8 was photographed at the Bracebridge terminal opposite the Gatehouse Hotel soon after entering service. It clearly depicts the lining of the beautiful pale green and cream livery.

MAURICE HODSON COLLECTION

This group photograph was taken inside the Bracebridge tramcar depot circa 1910. The depot could accommodate nine cars and it was extended in 1919 when three extra cars were added to the fleet.

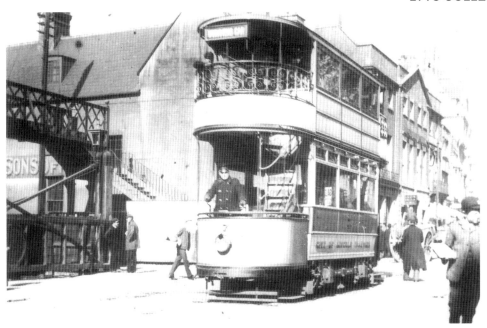

Brush car No 7 being worked on the Griffiths Bedell surface contact system passes over the Great Northern railway level crossing circa 1910-18. The large building in the background to the right of the tramcar and the building next to the railway footbridge were both demolished in 1970/71 to make way for the new inner City relief road, Wigford Way.

During the First World War, men were in short supply, so women crews were employed. Motorman Annie Scott, better known as Nancy was originally a cleaner at the Bracebridge depot and became probably the first woman tram driver in Great Britain. She is seen here with her conductress, at the controls of car No 2 standing at the Bracebridge terminal loop.

LVVS COLLECTION

Mr William Kirk stands proudly at the controls of tramcar No 7 as it arrives at the Bracebridge terminal. He started with the Corporation Tramways as a shed boy in 1915 and was promoted shortly afterwards at sixteen years of age, becoming the country's youngest ever tramway motorman. This photograph was taken in 1919 shortly before the route was converted to overhead power supply.

LVVS COLLECTION

The surface contact system was giving trouble as early as 1907. Tiny metal fragments including ladies' hairpins collected on the magnetic skates under the tramcars and caused short circuits. The decision was eventually taken to convert the system to conventional overhead power supply. The conversion took place in 1919 at a cost of £5,920 and it became operational on 26 December, Boxing Day, that same year. Some of the poles and wiring can be seen clearly in this photograph.

LVVS COLLECTION

Dick Kerr bodied car No 10 was one of three built in 1919 and supplied in battleship grey primer. They worked in service in this drab state for a short while before they received the pale green and cream livery. Motorman Annie Scott is at the controls as it heads through St Catherines, circa 1920.

Tramcar No 1, a Brush bodied Conaty & Lycett, passes St Catherine's church south bound for Bracebridge in 1921. It looks very different in this photograph having been fitted with its lower vestibules. Whilst this offered protection in inclement weather, the motormen frequently complained about the down draught as a result of the balconies not being enclosed.

Top covers were never fitted to tramcars No 2 and No 3 although vestibules were. Unlike all the other Brush bodied cars in the fleet these two also retained their original style, large piece top deck panels. This photograph was taken at the Bracebridge terminal loop, circa 1920/21.

Almost every motorman's favourite tramcar was No 6. With its lower end vestibules and fully enclosed balconies, better protection was given against bad weather. These modifications gave the car a modern streamlined appearance. Passing through St Catherine's in the early twenties it displays a revised destination blind. The St Benedict's title had been replaced by the new and more appropriate title, City.

LVVS COLLECTION

Vestibule car No 4 stands at the St Benedict's terminal in the City, circa 1928. On leaving the terminal the cars swung left into the first double track loop passing the Cornhill. The Stonebow archway beneath the Guildhall stands in the background and prevents any expansion of double deck tramcar operation any further due north.

LVVS COLLECTION

The last day of Tramcar operation, 4 March 1929, and Brush car No 6 built in 1905 stands aside the newest Leyland Titan TD1, No 34 (VL 1002) by the War Memorial on the High Street. Five cars departed from St Benedict's at 3.30 pm southbound for Bracebridge. The last car was No 6 which carried members of the City Council and the Transport Department. They returned to the City on motorbus No 34. Titan No 27 (VL 603) seen in the background was on service and had just returned from Monks Road.

DAILY MIRROR

PART 2 CITY OF LINCOLN OMNIBUSES

The first motorbuses were purchased by the Corporation in 1920/21. They were a batch of eleven Dennis, CAB model, normal control saloons with solid tyres. The handsome bodies were built by L L Motor Bodies of Louth, Lincolnshire and were of the rear entrance layout seating twenty-six passengers.

Slatted wooden seats were fitted forward and aft of a bulkhead thus dividing the saloon into two compartments with twelve seats in the forward section and fourteen in the rear.

The driver's cabin was full width, with a door on each side of the vehicle and one in the bulk-head through to the saloon. An extra seat was fitted alongside the driver and it was an honour for many schoolboys to "ride up front" with him.

Large route number boards were fitted on the roof at the front and rear with the destination names also displayed on boards beneath the side windows.

The fleet livery was light green body panels, cream window frames, white roofs and black mudguards. Large gold leaf fleet numbers shaded in black were applied and the company title, City of Lincoln Omnibuses also written in gold along the body side panels.

A new depot had been built on the Burton Road near Mount Street to house the new fleet of buses. The Manager of the Tramways, Mr Richard Hoggard appointed in October 1920 became the Manager at Burton Road on 10 January 1921 whilst still being the official manager of the Bracebridge depot. In practice, after the opening of the Burton Road depot the responsibility of running the tramway depot was in the hands of the experienced City Electrical Engineer, Mr Stanley Clegg.

The first three buses were delivered in 1920 and two began operation on 19 November that year on Route 1 to Burton Road. This was a circular service that ran in both directions. Burton Road via Cathedral anti-clockwise and Burton Road via West Parade clockwise. The route started from St Mary's Street adjacent to St Mary's Church and travelled via High Street, Silver Street, Lindum Road, Pottergate, Minster Yard, Priorygate, Eastgate, Bailgate, Newport, Rasen Lane, Burton Road, Yarborough Road, Hampton Street, West Parade, The Avenue, Newland, Mint Street (inward), High Street and St Mary's Street.

The clockwise service used the same roads with the exception of Mint Street, using Guildhall Street (outward).

Route 3 to Monks Road began in February 1921 and ran from St Mary's Street, via High Street, Silver Street, Monks Road terminating at Hartley Street.

In March 1921 a trial service to Wragby Road started running on Fridays and Saturdays only, to serve the new St Giles estate that was being built in the northeast part of the City.

The lengthy Burton Road circular route was split into two separate routes in April 1921. This became Route 1 Burton Road via Cathedral terminating at Mount Street and Route 2 West Parade terminating at the far end of the Parade. Route 2 was extended in May 1921 along Hewson Road terminating at the junction with Carholme Road. This replaced the City to Carholme Road service that was introduced a few months earlier.

The St Giles service proved viable and from July 1921 Route 5 was operating six days a week.

All the fleet of eleven new Dennis motorbuses were lined up on the cross roads of Burton Road/Yarborough Road for this photograph taken in 1921.

LVVS COLLECTION

Dennis CAB No 10 (FE 4092) seen outside the motor bodyworks of FM Thompson & Sons of Louth, prior to delivery. Note the additional nearside cab door. In 1928 this bus was converted for use as a lorry to carry coke from the gas works for firing the boiler in the St Marks depot.

R MARSHALL COLLECTION

The First City of Lincoln omnibus Dennis CAB No 1 (FE 3931). Probably taken in the summer of 1921/22 and about to depart on an outing. The side windows were detachable and some of them have been removed for the occasion. The wet weather canvas rolls can be seen at the top of each window aperture.

R MARSHALL COLLECTION

Housing development was taking place to a large extent on the southwest part of the city in the areas around the Newark Road, Skellingthorpe Road and Doddington Road during the 1920s.

Expansion was also taking place in the northern part of the city. The West Parade route became a circular service in April 1923 serving West Parade, Hewson Road and Carholme Road. The Monks Road service was extended from Hartley Street to terminate at Devon Street from November 1923. These changes as well as some increases in the frequency of the services led to the size of the fleet being increased.

Twelve new vehicles were added to the fleet during 1925-27, all of them single-deckers.

Four of these came from Guy Motors Ltd with the first two arriving in 1925 as Nos 12/13, (FE 6700/1). They were short wheelbase, normal control saloons and a considerable improvement on the earlier Dennis vehicles in that they were fitted with pneumatic tyres.

These smart little twenty-seaters, with bodies built in Lincoln by Bracebridge Motor Bodyworks, introduced one-man operation to the City for the first time when they began running on Route 4, from St Mary's Street to Doddington Road Bridge via Boultham Park Road, Rookery Lane, Newark Road and terminating at the junction of Doddington Road.

The next eight new buses came from Dennis and were the type E with pneumatic tyres, a longer wheel base and forward control layout allowing more room in the saloon for an increased seating capacity. These buses also had Bracebridge bodies and were given fleet numbers 14-21 and registered FE 8518-20/25-27 and FE 8870/71 when placed into service in 1926/27. Nos 20/21 were the pair that arrived in 1927.

The last of the twelve buses placed in service during the period 1925-27 were two Guy BB type, normal control saloons Nos 22/23 (FE 9806/7).

They were longer than the earlier two Guy buses and had a seating capacity of twenty-six.

Coachwork was by Bracebridge with forward exits, rear entrance layout and they were unique in having for the first time, moquette covered seats. Unlike the earlier pair of Guys these two were crew operated and initially worked on Route 6 to Swanpool. For a number of years prior to the Corporation operating the route, an independent operator Jack Corten, ran the service from Lincoln to Skellingthorpe village via Boultham Avenue and Boultham Park Road serving the Garden suburb of Swanpool on the Skellingthorpe road.

Mr Corten's service was taken over by City of Lincoln Omnibuses and he was given employment as a driver. The route then terminated at Swanpool.

The small Burton Road depot could not accommodate all of the fleet (by now 23 vehicles) at night and some buses had to be parked at Stores Park, land owned by the Royal Air Force adjacent to the small aerodrome, a quarter of a mile away on the Longdales Road. It became an inconvenience to have buses parked away from the depot so plans were made and approved to build a larger garage at St Marks Street in the City.

In April 1927 two new services were introduced from St Mary's Street, one to the new Barracks on the Burton Road via Yarborough Road. The second was a service to Nettleham Road/ Longdales Road junction via the Cathedral. They were numbered Routes 8 and 9 respectively.

No 12 (FE 6700) was one of a pair of Guy B type purchased in February 1925. They introduced one-man opera-
tion to the City when they commenced operation on Route 4, Doddington Road via Boultham Park Road and
Rookery Lane. They occasionally worked on other routes but latterly they were mainly to be found working on
Route 8, Yarborough Road.

R MARSHALL COLLECTION

The first Lincoln half-cab buses were the Dennis E type. The revolutionary new design gave the driver a separate cabin in the forward position at the side of the engine. This is No 14 (FE 8518), the first one to enter service
in August 1926. The batch had a short service life in Lincoln, being withdrawn at three years old and sold to
Cardiff Corporation Transport. They were replaced by the Thornycroft buses favoured by Mr Rock.

R MARSHALL COLLECTION

A broadside view of an unidentified Dennis E type which may have been taken on the Burton Road by the end of Olde Coach Road. The vehicle appears to have just been delivered by the coachbuilders to the Burton Road depot. It shows the elegance of the new, half-cab, rear entrance Bracebridge body.

LVVS COLLECTION

One of a pair of 26-seat Guy BB type, No 22 (FE 9806) had a dual doorway Bracebridge body. They were initially purchased for crew operation of Route 6 Swanpool but could be found occasionally on private hire work as seen in this photograph.

W J HAYNES

In September 1927 a Leyland Titan TD1 demonstration vehicle was used in a trial to determine whether or not a double decker could clearly pass underneath the Stonebow archway.

This vehicle owned by Leyland Motors and painted in a light blue and white livery had a lowbridge body with a sunken side gangway and an outside stairway mounted on an open rear platform.

The overall height of the bus was 12ft 10ins and it was able to pass under the Stonebow quite clearly.

At that year's Commercial Motor Show at Olympia in London, Leyland Motors displayed its first production model of the Titan TD1. Representatives of City of Lincoln Omnibuses visited the exhibition and after looking at the Titan expressed an interest in placing an order for ten double deckers to replace their tramcars. However, before ordering they asked if the one on display could be included in the purchase after the exhibition. Leyland agreed and so the order was placed.

The fine show bus joined the Lincoln fleet as No 24 (FE 9755) in December 1927. It too had a Leyland lowbridge body similar to the demonstrator. Its seating capacity was 48, twenty-four in each saloon. Each seat on the top deck sat four forward facing passengers on the left of the offside, sunken gangway. The seats were upholstered in green leather and the interior plywood side panels were covered with green Rexine. Ceilings were painted in white gloss. All the window frames and cills were beautifully finished in varnished, brown mahogany hardwood. Saloon ventilators were fitted above the top deck front windows and one in the lower deck bulkhead. These vents had a hinged wooden flap panel and could be opened and closed from the inside. Full drop side windows provided ventilation on the nearside and the lower deck, offside.

Two destination boxes were fitted, one in the piano style front, one at the rear above the platform. Power was supplied by a six cylinder 6.8 litre Leyland petrol engine on a low height chassis fitted with vacuum brakes made locally by Clayton Dewandre at the Titanic Works in Lincoln. These engineering developments helped to make the Leyland Titan TD1 a very successful modern double decker of the period.

At the time of No 24 going into service a batch of eight single deck Leyland Lion PLSC1 chassis was on order. Seven were to have bodywork built by Leyland. The first completed chassis of the batch however, was delivered to Bracebridge Bodyworks in Lincoln to receive its body. Fleet No 25 was reserved for it but whilst the Leyland bodies were being assembled it was decided to adopt a policy of reissuing fleet numbers vacated by displaced buses. The first four became Nos 1-3/6 (VL 300/600/01/04). The latter three of the batch were given the latest allocation of numbers 35-37 (VL 658-60), Nos 26-34 being reserved for the Titan double deckers undergoing assembly at that time. Lions No 1 and No 25 were the first two to be delivered to the Mount Street depot, entering service in March 1928. Their bodies were comparable, the Bracebridge body of No 25 (VL 77) was rather unique in having a smaller driver's cabin than the Leyland body and there was also an extra seat behind the front bulkhead.

The first ever double deck bus to pass underneath the Stonebow was a Leyland Titan TD1 (TD 9522) in September 1927. The bus owned by Leyland Motors was a demonstrator in a light blue and white livery. It was successfully trialled on the City routes and subsequently an order was placed at the Commercial Motor Show for a batch of ten buses.

City of Lincoln Omnibuses No 24 (FE 9755) was the first production Leyland Titan TD1. It was exhibited on the Leyland Motors stand at the 1927 Commercial Motor Show at Olympia, London. The livery was green, cream band relief with black lining and a white roof.

The first Leyland Lion PLSC1 to enter service was No 1 (VL 300) with Leyland 31 seat body. Originally it came as a forward entrance saloon in March 1928 but was converted to rear entrance layout soon after entering service.

Passing over the Skellingthorpe Road railway crossing during the 1930s is Leyland Lion PLSC1 No 37 (VL 660). It is on its way to the City and as the destination shows Burton Road, it is through working. This system known as the Spider plan of routes was introduced in May 1929 to offer passengers the facility to make across the City journeys. On this occasion it appears the gates are being worked manually by the permanent way staff.

The Leyland body of No 1 (VL 300) differed by having a forward entrance as opposed to a rear entrance. This layout was not repeated on the Lincoln Lions and No 1 remained a one-off until it was modified. Lions Nos 2/3/6 entered service in September 1928, Nos 35/36 in November and the last one No 37, in December 1928. The Titans Nos 26-28 (VL 602/3/5) also entered service in September 1928 and Nos 29-32 (VL 845-48) in December 1928. The last two Titans, Nos 33/34 (VL 1001/2), entered service in March 1929, timed to coincide with the closure of the tramway.

The new central depot at St Marks Street in Lincoln City centre opened on 7 November 1928. It was built on the site that was formerly the malleable ironworks of Harrisons and designed to accommodate fifty buses. There was also a small maintenance workshop with inspection pits.

The General Manager Mr Richard Hoggard put in his resignation to take effect from 31 January 1929 to take up a new post at Chesterfield. He was succeeded by Mr George Rock who was previously the General Manager at the West Monmouthshire Omnibus Board.

Another four new Lions entered service in June 1929 and had bodies built by Applewhite of Lincoln, on the slightly longer Leyland LT1 chassis. Leyland T type four cylinder petrol engines and four speed sliding mesh gearboxes were fitted. An extraordinary feature of these 33 seat rear entrance bodies was the use of mesh reinforced concrete to form the gangways instead of the standard tongued and grooved boards.

A notable feature in common with the earlier Leyland bodies was their grand style of roofs formed by steeply curved wooden ribs clad with narrow tongued and grooved wooden laths. The outside was covered with waterproofed "duck" cloth.

The saloons were furnished in a similar style to the earlier Lions and Titans. These buses replaced four of the Dennis CAB vehicles and took the numbers 4,5,7,8 and were registered VL 1262-65.

In May 1929 some cross-City journeys became available to passengers for the first time without the need to change at the St Mary's Street terminus. This allowed layover time in the City centre to be cut out. Initially, routes linked on weekdays were 3 (Monks Road) with 7 (Bracebridge); 5 (St Giles) with 4 and 6 (Swanpool and Doddington Road).

On Sundays only, Route 1 (Burton Road) was linked with 6 (Swanpool); 5 (St Giles) with 4 and 7 (Doddington Road and Bracebridge). Routes 3 (Monks Road) and 8 (Yarborough Road) remained separate on Sundays whilst Route 2 (West Parade) remained separate on all days. The Yarborough Road service was extended south to Scorer Street (off the High Street) for a trial period but proved unremunerative and was withdrawn in June 1929.

Leyland Lion PLSC1 No 25 (VL 77) was the "odd one out" amongst the Lions. It had a non-standard locally built, Bracebridge 32 seat body. An extra seat fitted behind the driver's cabin bulkhead was later removed as it obstructed the offside emergency exit. It became a 30 seater. The driver's cabin was slightly smaller than those of the Leyland bodies.

BRACEBRIDGE BODYWORKS/R MARSHALL COLLECTION

Leyland Titan TD1 No 30 (VL 846) stands at the Doddington Road terminus which from February 1928 was midway between the Newark Road and the Midland Railway crossing. The same spot today forms the junction with the Tritton Road. The crew in the picture were driver Bert Taylor who was later killed in the War and conductor Jack Hackney who became an inspector.

C V MIDDLETON

Passing through Pottergate Arch, the southern gateway of the Cathedral Close, is Leyland Lion LT1 No 5 (VL 1263). The bus, being driven here by former tramcar motorman Mr William Kirk, later passed to the City Engineer's Department for use as a snowplough in 1949. It was the first vehicle to be obtained by the Lincolnshire Vintage Vehicle Society in 1959 and was fully restored in 1984/85. Today it can be seen at the Society's Lincolnshire Road Transport Museum at North Hykeham, Lincoln.

LVVS COLLECTION

Applewhite Coachbuilders based in St Rumbold's Street, produced four bodies for Lincoln Corporation's Leyland Lions in 1929. No 4 (VL 1262) was the first of the batch, and in this photograph taken soon after entering service, it displays the new fleet name introduced by Mr Rock. The fleet number can be seen unusually on the lower part of the first near-side panel.

Leyland Lion LT1 No 7 (VL 1264) was one of four "long Lions" seating thirty-three. They were also known by the crews as the "fireproofs" as each had a concrete gangway. During the War they became standee buses with longitudinal seating, reverting to forward facing after the War. Here, it is doing a U turn on St Mary's Street to pull onto the City terminal by the church.

PART 3 LINCOLN CORPORATION TRANSPORT

Mr George Rock the General Manager and Engineer was influential in the purchase of six Thornycroft ZB6s with Bracebridge 32 seat rear entrance bodies added to the fleet during 1929. Nos 14-19 (VL 1906-11) came into service bearing the new fleet name, Lincoln Corporation Transport. This was contained in an attractive insignia with the City crest in the centre. It was designed by Mr Rock. Another new feature was the deep destination boxes for easier recognition. They were also fitted with non-fleet standard brown leather seats.

A new service to Westwick Drive via Moorland Avenue started in October 1929 initially on Fridays and Saturdays only.

At the outset of motorbuses being operated by the Corporation in 1920, some special services had been operated outside the City boundary. These were suspended in 1923 during consultations with the Minister of Transport. These services resumed in 1925 following approval by Lindsey County Council in accepting that the new pneumatic tyred buses were suitable for use on the county roads. All eleven Dennis CAB type buses had been equipped with the new pneumatic tyres.

An enquiry came from the LNER Company in October 1927 asking what powers the Corporation had to operate buses outside the City. An injunction to prevent them from doing so was not taken out following an agreement being reached, that specified the Corporation ran private parties only and was not allowed to advertise excursions. Kesteven County Council also refused to permit Corporation buses outside the City in November 1928 but relented three months later. This was in return for the Corporation agreeing to run specials only and drop the minimum fare conditions on other operators' buses entering the City. The Corporation began running Sunday circular tours during 1930. The fares were 6d for ten miles, 1/- for twenty miles and the tours soon proved popular. On the enforcement of the 1931 Road Traffic Act an application had to be made to continue running these services. Kesteven threatened to object unless the Corporation operated a service to North Hykeham. This was a reversal of their policies but the Traffic Commissioners refused to grant a licence for the service preferring instead an extension of Route 7 to the City boundary, in July 1931.

The number of passengers being carried had risen steadily throughout the 1920s but a new scale of higher fares introduced in September 1929 led to a decline in the number of passengers carried by March 1932. Unemployment in the heavy engineering industry was also a major factor.

Workmen's return tickets at cheap rates and shoppers' off-peak tickets had been available on the buses since 1926, and 1921 on the trams. Some variations in the cheap fare policy existed during 1930-32 but concessions were made extensively available from 1932 and thereafter the number of passengers carried began to rise.

Four of a batch of six Thornycroft ZB6s with bodywork built by Bracebridge Motor Bodyworks, stand outside the works prior to delivery in December 1929. On the left is No 17 (VL 1909) which was later used as an experimental vehicle when it was fitted with smaller pistons, small jets and large wheels. It wasn't a success, being very underpowered and unsuitable for working uphill routes due to overheating.

R MARSHALL COLLECTION

Standing outside the New Barracks of the Lincolnshire Regiment headquarters on Burton Road is Thornycroft ZB6 No 19 (VL 1911). This photograph of the elegant 32 seat saloon was probably taken on its first day in service. The new fleetname, Lincoln Corporation Transport, contained in an attractive insignia depicting a buckled belt with the City crest in the centre, designed by Mr Rock can be seen clearly.

C V MIDDLETON

Thornycroft ZB6 No 15 (VL 1907) is photographed beneath Pottergate Archway on a return journey to the City. The stone wall on the right of the picture was demolished in 1938 to allow double deck buses to pass on the correct side of the road. The archway then became an island and was closed to through traffic.

C V MIDDLETON

Two Thornycroft type BCs were purchased in 1932. Both were bodied in Lincoln but by different coachbuilders. No 38 (VL 4283) seen here was built by Bracebridge whilst No 39 (VL 4284) had a Rainforth body. There were some detail differences and the most obvious was the oddly shaped destination box fitted to No 39. These two buses were fitted with electric starters but these were later removed as drivers frequently broke them by not retarding the engine first. All of the Thornycrofts were prone to overheating and these two in particular were eventually fitted with wire grille bonnet sides. No 38 became an entertainment bus for ENSA during the Second World War to entertain service personnel stationed throughout Lincolnshire. It had a piano inside and curtains at the windows.

BRACEBRIDGE BODYWORKS, R MARSHALL COLLECTION

Two Thornycroft type BC were added to the fleet in 1932. Curiously one received a locally built body by Rainforth, No 38 (VL 4283) whilst the second received a Bracebridge body, No 39 (VL 4284).

Both vehicles had floating cabs, an unusual design allowing the structure of the driver's cabin to "float" above the chassis, thus minimising shock and vibration.

Expansion of services continued with two new routes being added in 1934. Route 7B Brant Road and Route 10 Rookery Lane both operated via the High Street. Increased frequencies on all routes, particularly on Fridays and Saturdays required a larger fleet leading to the purchase of seven second-hand buses during 1934. In May four Leyland Lions with London Midland and Scottish Railway 32 seat bodies were purchased from the LMSR. They were new in 1929, registered at Derby and were members of the Sheffield Joint Omnibus Committee, railway fleet. In the Lincoln fleet they became Nos 9/10/11/20 (CH 7915/07/05/08), each one having the Sheffield operator's blue moquette seats. Three Thornycroft type BC saloons with Vickers 32 seat bodies were acquired in November from the London and North Eastern Railway company. These were also ex-members of the Sheffield Joint Omnibus Committee, railway fleet and were full fronted vehicles with forward entrances and maroon leather seats. Each one was fitted with a roof luggage rack and a ladder at the rear.

These three buses were in railway livery and in a very bad condition when they arrived from Sheffield, and as well as putting them in order it was necessary to convert each one to half cab, rear entrance configuration prior to them entering service. They became Lincoln Nos 13/21/40, (UU 8886/92/90) and were the last single deckers to be put into service during the pre-war period of rapid expansion.

Mr George Rock, the General Manager and Engineer introduced several mechanical and other innovations during the 1930s. In 1933 six Verometer ticket roll machines were purchased. These experimental examples, made locally by Clayton Dewandre, proved successful and from January 1934 all conductors were issued with them.

The Leyland Titan TD1 buses proved to be very reliable in service and therefore it was not surprising that the second order for double deckers went to Leyland. This was a small order of four new buses to be built, again with Leyland bodies but this time highbridge type with a modern enclosed stairway on the Titan TD4 chassis introduced by Leyland in 1935. A choice of engines was offered for this chassis, the 8.8 litre petrol or the 8.6 litre oil engine. Lincoln Corporation chose oil engines.

These four handsome looking buses were constructed with metal body frames. They had a capacity of 56 and the seats were covered with green leather. The interior colour scheme was similar to that of the Lions and TD1s with green sides, white ceilings and brown linoleum floor coverings. Metal tread plates fixed on the floor between the seats were introduced in place of the traditional wooden laths. All the interior lights were fitted with "butter dish" style lamp globes.

They were Nos 41-44 (VL 8845-48) and were placed into service in December 1936 wearing the same livery as the earlier double deckers, green lower and upper panels relieved by three cream bands with black lining. The roofs were painted white.

Another photograph of No 15 (VL 1907) shows it about to depart from one of the City outer terminals, possibly St Giles or Rookery Lane. The conductor equipped with a Verometer ticket machine looks set to give the driver a bell signal to move off.

CLAYTON DEWANDRE, R MARSHALL COLLECTION

Lincoln's first diesel oil engined buses were placed into service in December 1936. They were also innovative in being the first metal-framed buses built for Lincoln and to a highbridge height of 14ft 3ins. The road surface beneath the Stonebow had to be lowered for these four new buses to pass clearly through the archway. As can be seen in this Leyland Motors photograph taken in November 1936, the vehicle was unregistered and without a fleet number. It became No 41 (VL 8845).

LEYLAND MOTORS, R MARSHALL COLLECTION

The Leyland TD5 was introduced to the Lincoln fleet in 1937 with a batch of six. They had Leyland all metal bodies similar to the earlier batch of four Leyland TD4s. In this photograph No 49 (AFE 85), wearing the green, three cream band livery with black horizontal mouldings is captured passing the Saracen's Head Hotel on the High Street.

W J HAYNES

Leyland Titan TD5 No 57 (AFE 376) was one of the second batch of TD5s, supplied in March/ April 1938. It stands outside the then recently extended offices of the Transport Department, circa 1939, in original pre-war livery.

THE OMNIBUS SOCIETY

During 1936 an application was made to the Traffic Commissioners to operate a route to Cherry Willingham, a village on the north east side of the City but this was turned down. However, passenger numbers continued to increase on the established routes and an extra six double deckers were required for delivery during 1937.

The Titan TD4 had only a short production run which ended when Leyland Motors introduced its succeeding model, the TD5 in 1937. Lincoln Corporation became one of the first operators to place an order for the new Titan model.

The six buses Nos 45-50 (AFE 31-33/84-86) were put on the road in October 1937. Twelve more were ordered for delivery in 1938/39. They became Nos 51-60 (AFE 370-72/ 69/73/74/76/75/77/78) delivered in March and April 1938. In March 1939 Nos 61/62 (AVL 409/10) were delivered.

They were all very similar in appearance to the earlier TD4 buses. The interior colour scheme and the external livery were also the same. Metal framed bodywork was again by Leyland, seating 56. All eighteen had the 8.6 litre oil engine. During 1938, six Lions and six Thornycrofts were ousted by the new Titans. The withdrawn buses were parked on the railway sidings by the road known as the Ropewalk, near the St Marks depot.

Some minor service changes occurred in April 1938. The Nettleham Road service No 9 having previously been extended in 1933 to terminate at Swift Gardens on the St Giles Estate, became a circular service. This was made possible by the completion of the new Outer Circle Drive linking up to the Wragby Road for the return to the City. Service No 5, St Giles via Wragby Road ran anti-clockwise along the Outer Circle and returned to the City along the Nettleham Road.

A new service, Cannon Street – Scorer Street was introduced but withdrawn on 5 November the same year due to poor revenue.

The layout of the St Marks garage was somewhat unsatisfactory in its as-built form. The opportunity was taken to extend the garage at the rear right hand side on land formerly occupied by a row of terrace houses. The extension housed a new workshop thus releasing the former workshop area for parking. The new workshop was designed by Mr Rock and innovative in being the first of its kind in the country to have the workshop area and the buses on two levels. This made inspection and maintenance easier by cutting out the inconvenience of climbing in and out of the service pits. The extension opened on 18 March 1939. A point of interest is that the depot was often hired out for boxing matches and public meetings. On those occasions some buses not in service were parked outside.

The outbreak of war in September 1939 led to services being curtailed and during the following years there was the drive to save fuel when rationing was introduced. The pressure to maintain services meant that a staggered hours system of operation was introduced on 1 January 1942. Mr Rock explored the possibilities of some of the buses running on town gas. This employed a gas compressor and small cylinders capable of storing gas at 3,000 lbs psi. Approval was given to go ahead but the gas compressor that was purchased was unsatisfactory so the scheme was abandoned.

Increased traffic numbers led to the four withdrawn long Lions being re-instated for service. Each one was converted to form a standee vehicle with perimeter seats.

The photographer was poised on the steps of the Great Northern railway footbridge to capture this charming photograph of Leyland TD5 No 58 (AFE 375) as it passed over the level crossing.

G H F ATKINS VIA/LVVS COLLECTION

This pre-delivery photograph shows the superb styling and craftsmanship of the late nineteen thirties Leyland coachwork. This Titan (registered AVL 409) became No 61 and it was Lincoln's penultimate TD5, entering service in March 1939. It has a white roof here but silver roofs were introduced later to the one cream band livery, from about 1948, and only on the Titan classes TD1, TD4 and TD5s.

LEYLAND MOTORS, LVVS COLLECTION

34

A view across the new workshop shows the split level floor. It was designed by Mr Rock to give easy walk-in access to each of the five inspection pits. In the background can be seen the body repair workshop on the left and to the right is the paint shop.

LVVS COLLECTION

This interesting photograph taken inside the St Marks depot in February 1954 offers another view looking over the basement level workshop. In the foreground can be seen the two cranes which evolved from improvisation plans of Mr Rock's. The stanchions were disused tramway standards. The jib arms were composed from part of a scrapped Thornycroft back axle, capable of rotating 360 degrees and carrying a Morris runway type block and tackle. This overcame the difficulty initially experienced in raising and lowering engines at overhaul between the two floor levels.

LINCOLNSHIRE ECHO
Ri/1684A.jpg

Four Leyland Titan TD7 chassis were ordered in 1940 but only two were manufactured due to restrictions imposed by the Ministry of Supply, a Government body. As a result, all bus production throughout Great Britain tailed off by early 1941 so that manufacturers, including Leyland Motors, could put their factories into military production.

Many bus companies incurred heavy losses of vehicles during 1940/41 and so the Ministry lifted restrictions towards the end of 1941 and allowed Leyland components held in store and termed "frozen" pending assembly, to be "unfrozen" and assembled.

The two Leyland TD7 chassis for Lincoln Corporation were assembled prior to the end of 1940 and so were not unfrozen examples. Leyland bodies are thought to have been ordered but for some unknown reason the Lincoln pair was sent to Charles H Roe coachbuilders at Leeds and received two elegant bodies similar in appearance to the earlier Leyland TD5 bodywork.

These two buses Nos 63/64 (BFE 418/19) were the first Roe bodied buses to be supplied to Lincoln. Teak wood was used to construct the framework with sliding windows to provide ventilation. Roofs were single skin, pressed steel panels with a notably steep contour reminiscent of earlier railway carriages. Inside the saloons, the colour scheme was in keeping with earlier vehicles. Dark mahogany was used on the window cills and frames. Wooden tread laths were fixed to the floor between the seats. Seating capacity was for 56 passengers (30 upper saloon, 26 lower saloon) on green crocodile skin pattern, leather seats with rectangular shaped back rests. Hand grabs and rails were clad in black plastic. Nos 63/64 were completed in February 1941.

No Lincoln buses were destroyed during wartime air raids but new buses were needed to replace the second-hand single deckers withdrawn in 1940. In 1942 Guy Motors of Wolverhampton was given the authorization to manufacture double deck bus chassis. The Arab Mk II could be supplied with a five or six cylinder Gardner LW engine. Various body builders took part in supplying the utility bodies to a standard Ministry of Supply design. Lincoln Corporation ordered a batch of ten of these utility Arabs to be supplied from 1943 onwards. The first one to arrive, No 65 (BFE 420) was fitted with a five cylinder engine but was unable to cope with Lindum Hill when fully laden. On these occasions some passengers were requested to get off the bus at the top of Lindum Road and walk the remaining part of the hill to Minster Yard where they would re-board for the remainder of their journey.

Five Arabs were delivered in 1943/44 and they were Nos 66 (BFE 421), 10-13 (BVL 7/8/24/52). As a result of the experiences with No 65 Lincoln was allowed to obtain six-cylinder Gardner engines for these and the remaining four buses of the order. The Park Royal bodies were framed with unseasoned English ash hardwood clad with steel panels and they had very distinctive raked fronts that were common to the war period. The saloons were very basic and did not have interior side panels. The lower deck ceilings were panelled with hardboard whilst the roofs were single skin steel panels, brass riveted to exterior right angle section steel ribs.

Four Leyland TD7s with Leyland bodywork were originally ordered but due to wartime restrictions only two chassis were supplied. The order for bodywork was passed to Charles H Roe of Leeds. The first one, No 63 (BFE 418) stands in the snow in February 1941, outside the Crossgates Carriage works awaiting delivery wearing a wartime version of the Lincoln green and cream livery. To comply with wartime regulations the traditional white roofs were not allowed, so green was chosen.

CHARLES. H. ROE / R. MARSHALL COLLECTION

Resurfacing work was being carried out on Burton Road when this picture was taken of No 64 (BFE 419) on 30 March 1953. The mid war/early post war livery of green with one cream band was rather drab compared to the beautiful three cream band, black lined livery of earlier years. This bus was purchased in 1963 by Mr F V Le Tall, founder member of the Lincolnshire Vintage Vehicle Society. On his death in 1989 the bus was bequeathed to the Society and now forms part of the "Le Tall Collection" of vehicles.

LINCOLNSHIRE ECHO
Ri/1465

Guy Arabs joined the fleet during the war years. The first one to enter service was No 65 (BFE 420) in July 1943. It was originally fitted with a five cylinder Gardner LW engine, but this proved unsuitable and it was refitted with a 6LW engine in May 1948, shortly before this photograph was taken on 4 June. This bus and No 66 had unusual gear boxes. The gear positions were back to front and identified by a red knob on the gear stick.

R MARSHALL

Passing by the Treaty of Commerce public house on the High Street on 18 March 1950 is Guy Arab No 66 (BFE 421). The livery seen here was introduced with the arrival of the Guys in 1943. At the end of the war some of them appeared in a two cream band variation. This one though retained its single cream band including the black lining throughout its time in service.

R MARSHALL

These six buses were all built to full utility standard comprising wooden slatted seats and had a capacity of 56. The latter four of the batch Nos 14-17 (BVL 162/319/320/398) delivered in 1945 were semi-utility having seats made up of canvas and moquette of a very rough quality. This was a sharp contrast in comfort to the wooden seats due to the partial relaxation of restrictions governing vehicle manufacture. Ventilation was rather poor, provided by an insufficient amount of half-drop side windows and saloon ventilators at the front.

All the stanchion poles, staircase hand rails and platform grabs were steel, clad in plastic. The short ceiling rails to the rear of the lower saloon were made of hardwood.

Only one destination box was permitted in the construction and the rear registration numbers were painted on the platform window glass.

All the saloon lights were fitted with charming "butter dish" style globes like those first introduced in 1936 on the Titans Nos 41-44.

After the war five new double deckers were ordered from Leyland Motors to increase the size of the fleet. These were the PD1 Titans powered by Leyland 7.4 litre, six cylinder oil engines coupled to a four-speed constant mesh gearbox. Triple servo brakes were fitted.

The complete vehicle was available from Leyland but Lincoln Corporation opted for coachwork built by Charles H Roe of Leeds.

Nos 18-22 (BVL 720-724, not in numerical order) entered service in July 1946 and were followed by five more, 67-71 (CFE 563-567) in July 1947. These five were of the type classified by Leyland as the PD1A. Mechanically the only difference from the PD1 was that the PD1A had rubber bushes on the road spring shackle pins whereas the PD1 had metal bushes.

The teak framed highbridge bodies were similar on both batches supplied to Lincoln. The saloons were fitted in similar style as the earlier buses 63/64. The seat backs had a slightly curved stainless steel top edge instead of being square and the hand grabs and rails were stainless steel.

Seating capacity was again for 56 passengers, set out 31 above 25 inside, again in green crocodile leather but this time in the rib style of upholstery. The rear seat upstairs sat three and the two side seats downstairs over the wheel arches sat three on the near and two on the offsides.

Three more PD1A buses were ordered and these were Nos 72-74 (CVL 770-772) entering service on 3 April 1948. One detail in particular shone them out from the previous ten Roe bodies. This was the kidney bean shaped window on the staircase but apart from that they were almost the same.

To mark the end of World War II and the announcement of Victory, one of the new Guy Arabs was painted in a special livery designed by General Manager Mr George Rock. This is No 14 (BVL 162) captured passing the St Peter in Eastgate church on a journey to the St Giles estate in 1945. Later in its working life this bus was fitted with an experimental braking system in collaboration with the Lincoln based manufacturer, Clayton Dewandre.

LINCOLNSHIRE ECHO
Ri/555A

Five Charles H Roe bodied Leyland Titan PD1s were Lincoln's first post-war delivery of buses. They entered service in July 1946. The third one of the batch No 20 (BVL 720) was nearly four years old at the time this photograph was taken next to St Mary's church on 18 March 1950. Note the beautiful chrome plated radiator shell.

R MARSHALL

Priorygate Archway is the northern gateway of the Cathedral Close. Roe bodied Leyland Titan PD1A No 69 (CFE 565) new in July 1947, passes carefully through the arch on a journey to Burton Road on 10 August 1952.

R MARSHALL

It is evident by the gleaming front wings and headlamps that PD1A No 70 (CFE 566) had recently entered service when this picture was taken in the Rookery Lane area. The narrow, non-standard width, single cream band appears to have been applied only to No 70 and the other four buses in the 1947 batch.

W J HAYNES

Whilst these buses were robust in their construction, the adoption of the 7.4 litre engine was a retrograde step in terms of development. Their performance in top gear was good and reliability excellent but they were poor at pulling away when moderately loaded and were also notorious for being slow through the gears. When they pulled away with a fair load and also when ascending Lindum Hill and the long climb up the Yarborough Road, their engines droned. This deep throaty sound was to be heard at its best in congested City traffic during hot summer days when the engines were hot and the air humid.

Towards the end of 1948 another batch of double deckers was put into service. These were the Guy Arab Mk III with Gardner 6LW engines, four speed constant mesh gearboxes and vacuum assisted hydraulically operated brakes. The first one of the batch to be completed was No 23 (DFE 383) and it was displayed by Guy Motors on their stand at the 1948 Commercial Motor Show. Unlike the other nine buses of the batch, No 23 was fitted with a Meadows 6DC630 engine of 10.35 litre capacity.

The bodywork was also manufactured by Guy using Park Royal components throughout including, for example, the window casings which were pressed steel. The use of overlap rubber channel eliminated internal window ledges. Each window was trimmed with green and cream Rexine. The green surrounded the lower half of the window, matching the green painted single skin body panels. Ceilings were painted cream and the seats were again covered in green leather but this time fashioned in the earlier style of flat cushions with ribbed back rests, giving a capacity of 56 with 30 on the upper deck and 26 on the lower.

The hand grab rails on the rear platform of No 23 contained a safety mechanism devised by Mr Rock. In the event of a passenger being dragged along the road, the resultant downward force on the rail would trigger a red warning light in the driver's cabin. This experimental system was not a success due to abuse by some passengers boarding the vehicle whilst it was clearly pulling away. It was therefore not fitted to any of the other vehicles in the fleet. Older buses that had been withdrawn from service had once again left fleet numbers vacant in the series so these new deckers were given reissued numbers, 1-3/23/35-40 (DFE 384-86/83/87/446-48/523/24).

The number of passengers carried in 1939 was 9.7 million, rising to 16.3 m in 1945 and 18.8 m in 1949. Services had expanded to cope with the demand and as such 19.8m were carried in 1952. This was to remain the highest number of passengers carried in any one year. Special works services were also increased from 1945 and in response to several requests from groups of employees at local factories, direct works specials were introduced. These included, Robeys, Ruston & Hornsbys, Newsums Joinery, Ruston Bucyrus and Clayton Dewandre. Housing development continued in various parts of the City after the war. In the south of the City the Boultham Moor Estate was under construction on the land bounded by the Skellingthorpe Road and Doddington Road. To serve this estate the Corporation introduced service No 12, Boultham Moor via Dixon Street and the Boultham Park Road in August 1947.

In January 1948 two routes were revised. This allowed Route 3 to be extended from Sherbrooke Street to the Tower Estate. Route 5 originally running via Pottergate, Eastgate and Langworthgate was now to be rerouted onto the Wragby Road at the Pottergate junction and then to run via Queensway to serve the County Hospital and HM Prison. The St Georges Hospital on the Long Leys Road received a service for the first time from 13 November 1950. A year earlier Route 4 was extended along the Doddington Road several journeys a day to terminate at Whisby Road. This was to serve the people living in temporary ex-RAF buildings on the Skellingthorpe Aerodrome. Further changes took place in 1950, the first being Route 2, West Parade. It was given cross-the-town status when it was linked to serve Scorer Street and St Andrews Street, just off the lower part of the High Street.

In April that year Sunday morning services were re-introduced and the popular Circular Tours into the countryside were re-introduced the following month.

A lovely view of an almost new Leyland Titan PD1A No 72 (CVL 770) as it passes along St Mary's Street on 4 June 1948 to take up its position on the Rookery Lane stand by the church. Note the charming kidney bean shape staircase window of the 1948 Roe body.

R MARSHALL

Leyland Titan TD4 No 42 (VL 8846) is seen at the City terminus by St Mary's church, now wearing the mid-war years introduction of green with one cream band livery, in the autumn on 17 October 1948.

R MARSHALL

30 November 1948 was the first day in service for a special new bus. No 23 (DFE 383) was a Guy Arab III fitted with a non standard Meadows 6DC630 type engine. The safety grab handles on the rear platform were designed by Mr Rock and these contained intricate cured wiring manufactured by Jointine Products of Tanners Lane, Lincoln. In the unfortunate event of a passenger being dragged along the road, the downward force on the hand grab would trigger a red warning light in the driver's cabin. Rubber bell strip was fitted on the ceilings of both saloons and when pressed a blue warning light would illuminate in the driver's cabin. Prior to delivery No 23 featured on the Guy Motors stand at the 1948 Commercial Motor Show at London in the austere postwar, green with one cream band livery.

LINCOLNSHIRE ECHO
Ri/636B

The last Guy Arab to enter service was No 40 (DFE 524) in June 1949. This picture taken after a heavy snow-fall in January 1956 shows the buses still managed to get through. No 40 turns carefully out of Pottergate to descend Lindum Road. The large gable ended building in the background is Lincoln's oldest public house, The Adam and Eve.

LINCOLNSHIRE ECHO
Ri/2551

All ten of the Leyland Titan TD1 buses were refurbished to extend their service lives. The upper deck floors and the cabs were prone to sagging due to inadequate ceiling ribs. Some were done in the St Marks bodyshop and some by Bracebridge bodyworks. They were also upgraded to a seating capacity of 51 by the addition of a bench seat for three passengers at the rear of the upper saloon. Those refurbished after the War were repainted with a silver roof as seen in this photograph of No 28 (VL 605) on St Mary's Street on 4 June 1948.

R MARSHALL

The first Leyland Titan PD2/10 to be delivered was No 31 (EVL 544) and captured by the Lincolnshire Echo photographer in the St Marks depot. It is awaiting its early morning crew to be taken into service on its first day 15 September 1951.

LINCOLNSHIRE ECHO
Ri/873

PART 4 CITY OF LINCOLN

In September 1951 the first of a batch of ten new double deckers was placed into service; the rest followed in October and November.

They were Leyland Titan PD2/10 with Roe highbridge teak framed bodies, Nos 24-33 (EVL 537-46) with Leyland 0600 type engines. These fine buses replaced the ageing TD1 buses that were maintained in active service for far longer than originally intended due to the effects imposed by World War II.

Two of the TD1s went out for scrap in 1948 and those were ironically the youngest of the batch, Nos 33/34, whist some soldiered on to become twenty two/three years old by the time that they were ousted by the new Titans in 1950/51.

The Roe bodywork of Nos 24-33 could well be called a classical style of the period with the slightly raked front, steeply curved roof domes and deep windows.

Inside they were furnished in the same beautiful style and colour as the earlier Titan PD1 bodies. The seating capacity and style of seats was also the same, 30 upstairs, 26 below.

Stopping indicators were fitted on the lower saloon bulkhead panel and above the front windows of the upper saloon. The orange glass panel displayed the word "stopping" in black capital letters and became illuminated each time the rubber stopping strip was pressed. These indicators worked in conjunction with a buzzer in the driver's cabin.

The visual display indicated that the bus was about to stop and should have prevented passengers wishing to alight giving the driver a repeated signal.

Unfortunately this was not always the case and complications arose due in part to there being some compulsory bus stops in various parts of the City. Drivers would observe these compulsory stopping places unless the conductors signalled twice to carry on. Allowing passengers the privilege to give the stopping signal sometimes resulted in a bus not stopping at a compulsory stop due to the stop strip being pressed twice. This signal system was devised by Mr Rock and it was his last innovation before taking his retirement. It followed earlier experiments on Guy 23 which was prepared for the 1948 Commercial Motor Show. The system on No 23 employed a bell strip on the ceilings and blue and green stop and go signal lights in the driver's cabin.

Mr Rock was succeeded by Mr F Frazer in 1951 and soon after taking up office he purchased a 1938 Leyland Cub in October 1951 from the Lincolnshire Road Car Company in whose fleet it had been No 540 (ABE 347). The 20 seat forward entrance body built by Brush was painted light green and numbered 5. It was used on the West Parade and the St Georges/City Hospital routes and also used by the City Council for inspecting the Council-owned allotments.

The Verometer ticket machines in general use from 1934-45 were withdrawn due to spare parts becoming unobtainable when Clayton Dewandre ended production of the model.

The Department reverted to Bell Punch tickets until 1952 when "Ultimate" ticket machines were purchased. This model issued pre-printed paper tickets from a roll by pressing down quick release levers to eject the tickets to be torn from the corresponding roll. This type of machine was extremely reliable and efficient allowing the conductor to collect the fares very quickly, particularly at peak times.

Taking up its position to pass beneath the Stonebow Archway from where this photograph was taken on 14 October 1952 is Leyland Titan PD2/10 No 27 (EVL 540). It is followed by Leyland Titan PD1A No 73 (CVL 771). Another PD2 can be seen in the background at the bus stand by the War Memorial. The High Street is crowded with shoppers, and judging by their overcoats its was quite a cold day.

LINCOLNSHIRE ECHO
Ri/663A/1

When just four years old Guy Arab No 23 (DFE 383) was fitted with a Leyland 8.6 engine. The Leyland unit was slightly longer than the original Meadows engine, and this is evident by the radiator protruding ahead of the cab front. Compare this photograph with that of the previous page. Records show that the Leyland engine was fitted in February 1953. The two cream band livery seen here was adapted to the Guys only. It was introduced in 1945 on some of the utilities and then in 1952-54 on the first six Arab Mk III buses.

R MARSHALL COLLECTION

A Land Rover purchased in 1952 ably demonstrates its pulling power on the 1 in 9 gradient of Lindum Road. It served in the capacity of a recovery vehicle for ten years. The vehicle being towed is No 54, one of the 1938 Leyland TD5 class in March 1953. For some obscure reason, route number binds were discontinued by General Manager Mr Frazer from 1951 onwards and the absence of a blind is clear in this photograph.

LINCOLNSHIRE ECHO
Ri/2058B

Looking resplendent in the Coronation special livery on 30 May 1953 is Guy Arab III, No 3 (DFE 386). The bus was in regular service and special souvenir tickets were issued to passengers. After the celebration period the Royal Insignia and garlands were removed and the bus then ran for quite some time in plain cream livery before being repainted into fleet livery.

LINCOLNSHIRE ECHO
Ri/886

In the north of the City, the planned large Ermine Estate at Riseholme was being built. In 1952 service 8 which terminated at the Longdales Road roundabout was rerouted to turn off that road just short of the roundabout, into the new Ravendale Drive, turning left onto Laughton Way and terminate at Broxholme Gardens. As development of the estate continued apace, the route eventually became 8A and 8B turning left and right respectively onto the Laughton Way thus providing a full circle coverage of the whole estate.

Changes were also made to the Swanpool Route 6 when alternate journeys were routed via Hemswell Avenue to serve the Hartsholme Estate on the Skellingthorpe Road.

The Doddington Road/Whisby Road Route 4A was revised in 1952 to terminate at Whitley Way, providing an improved service for the people living in the hutments on the south side of the large Skellingthorpe Aerodrome. It operated every two hours via Canwick Road and South Park in conjunction with a new South Park circular service from the City via Canwick Road, South Park and High Street. This also operated every two hours alternately with the 4A, thus it gave an hourly frequency and provided a service to the South Park area of the City for the very first time. It operated until 1956 when the new South Park Avenue was built. This new road cut across the line of the South Park roadway and the eastern half of the original road became a block end.

General Manager Mr Frazer resigned his post in June 1953 to take up a position with Aberdeen Corporation Transport.

He was succeeded by Mr Herbert Jones, previously with Leigh Corporation Transport.

To commemorate the Coronation of Her Majesty, Queen Elizabeth II, Mr Frazer had authorised a double decker to be painted in a special commemorative livery of all over cream. The bus chosen was Guy Arab No 3 and it worked on all the City Routes. Souvenir tickets were issued to passengers riding on the special bus.

The following year (1954), Leyland PD1A No 67 was painted in similar livery to commemorate the 50th year of municipal transport in Lincoln.

It was decided in 1954 to put back on the road the utility Guy Arabs that had been laid up in the back of the garage for quite some time due to their inferior body frames.

Between 1954 and 56 each one in turn had its framework stripped of the steel panelling and then reframed with good quality timber and included sliding vent windows to replace the inadequate number of the half drop type. An extra destination box was fitted above the rear platform.

Nos 65/10-13 on completion, received seats removed from previously withdrawn TD4 and TD5 buses.

No 66 was the only one of the batch not refurbished, having been withdrawn and cannibalised for spare parts in September 1954.

To commemorate the fiftieth anniversary of municipal transport in Lincoln, Leyland Titan PD1A No 67 (CFE 563) was painted in a special livery. It comprised cream as the main colour with three green bands.

LVVS COLLECTION

The Coronation special livery was clearly the inspiration that led to the buses being brightened up with the introduction of a new livery. This comprised a broader amount of cream than all the previous liveries. A change of paint suppliers resulted in a lighter shade of green being obtained but it was decided to use it as a trial to see if it would enhance the cream. No 3 was the first bus to receive the new livery. However, the pea green did not find favour and it was very soon repainted into the correct Lincoln green, as it appears in this photograph.

R.H.G. SIMPSON COLLECTION

Guy Arab No 66 (BFE 421) new in August 1943 was not selected for rebuilding and so had a rather short service life, being withdrawn at 11 years old and then cannibalised for mechanical parts. It passed to a south Lincolnshire farmer for use as a store shed and later in 1967, it was rescued for preservation by the author. Unfortunately the project was abandoned in 1971 after a severe gale force wind inflicted huge damage taking off the roof and top deck sides. This photograph was taken on 12 March 1967.

STEVE MILNER

The ten utility Guy Arab buses supplied during 1943-46 were built with inferior unseasoned English ash timber and as a result became unserviceable after a few years. During 1954-56 nine of them were rebuilt in the St Marks workshop. This picture taken on 3 February 1955 shows No 11 (BVL 8) undergoing the work. The additional sliding vent, window rail is in situ on the nearside indicating that reframing on that side is complete whilst work on the offside has yet to begin. With the exception of the original steel roof they were repanelled in aluminium.

LINCOLNSHIRE ECHO
RI/1009

Some of the Leyland TD5 buses were repainted in a revision of the green with three cream band livery during 1953/54. The silver roofs were omitted in preference for green. There were other variations occurring from time to time, possibly for the creation of a new livery. This included some members of the Roe bodied PD1 and PD2/10 classes which received a narrow cream band or bands not in keeping with the standard livery.

Leyland TD5 No 46 wore an arrangement of cream window frames with a cream waist and the cant rail also in cream. The lower panels, upper panels and roof were in green.

The popularity of the special commemorative liveries applied to No 3 and No 67 had created a desire within the Transport Department to produce a modern, brighter livery. In the summertime of 1954 Guy Arab No 3 was repainted in a new bright livery which contained a large amount of cream similar to the Coronation special livery. The lower panels and roof were painted in green whilst the upper panels and window frames were in cream.

A change to a different paint supplier led to a lighter shade of green being obtained. This pea green was applied to No 3 but it wasn't very well liked and it was very soon repainted into the correct shade of Lincoln green.

An original example of one of the Coronation bus tickets issued during June 1953.

COURTESY OF TOM FREEMAN

An example of an Ultimate ticket. These type of tickets were introduced in 1952.

CYRIL COOKE COLLECTION

For many years the City bus services were severely disrupted by the two railway crossings on the High Street and also the railway crossing on Pelham Street. The frequency of goods trains of both the Great Northern and the Midland railways passing through the Pelham junction caused many delays. The volume of traffic using the High Street was also adding to the problem. A new flyover bridge spanning the busy railway junction was proposed to reduce the hold-ups. After years of planning it was finally given the go ahead with the project being formally announced in July 1954. However, in October 1955 work on the bridge had still not begun, so Lincoln MP Mr Geoffrey de Freitas raised the point with the Minister of Transport. He asked if the project was being held up due to national budget cuts. The reply was that there was no reason for any delay, and with that result the project began in January 1956, with the demolition of rows of houses and many other buildings on Melville Street, Pelham Street, Canwick Road, Norman Street, Napoleon Place and Oxford Street. It was a redevelopment on a huge scale and to coincide with the new bridge the Corporation purchased a part of the Great Northern station car park from British Railways and widened the roadway on St Mary's Street. Three new concrete bus shelters were erected and this formed the first phase of the new bus terminal for services to the south of the City. It became operational in 1953 and the old shelters by the church were then removed. Three additional shelters formed phase two and they were erected at the eastern end of St Mary's Street opposite both the Grand and Oxford hotels. The shelters on the High Street opposite the Cornhill were then removed, and from 1957 the northern services departed from the first three forward shelters whilst the southern departures were transferred once again, to the three rear shelters.

Work on the flyover bridge continued throughout 1957 and roused a great deal of interest and debate, in particular what the bridge should be named. Many suggestions were put forward, the favourite being Lindum. Others included Cathedral Approach as the bridge would offer stunning views of the Cathedral. Minster, St Andrews (from the nearby church of that name). Oxhill was another with "Ox" taken from Oxford Street and "hill" from Alderman Hill, the Chairman of the City Council's level crossings committee. Ruston was suggested due to the bridge's close proximity to the iron works of Ruston and Hornsby. An unusual one was Stoparc, suggested by a local newspaper correspondent. It translated as Solving Temporarily Our Problems Against Railway Crossings. Eventually the name Pelham was chosen and this reflected the street of the same name which part of the length of the bridge would run adjacent.

Pelham Bridge opened for use on 10 December 1957 and was officially opened by Her Majesty the Queen on 27 June 1958.

Taken in the early spring sunshine on 15 April 1955 against the background of the tall Albion Hotel is recently rebuilt Utility Guy Arab No 10 (BVL 7). The insertion of sliding vent windows and the introduction of the new broad cream and green livery gave the utility bodies a more up to date appearance.

R MARSHALL

Lincoln's first utility bus, Guy Arab No 65 (BFE 420) was originally supplied in the wartime, one cream band, green livery. By the time this photograph was taken on 13 June 1960, it had been renovated and the steel lower deck panels had been replaced with aluminium. Unlike the others of the batch, it retained its four utility quota drop windows but its utility wooden seats were replaced. In 1962 No 65 had the top deck removed, the chassis shortened and it became a break down lorry for the Lincoln fleet. It served admirably in that role until February 1975.

GERALD MEAD

This photograph shows a typical hold-up at the busy Durham Ox level crossing on Pelham Street and the need for a new flyover road bridge. It was taken in January 1956 just before the demolition work began on the public house that same month. Demolition then followed on many other buildings in the path of the bridge.

MAURICE HODSON COLLECTION

Picture taken on 5 October 1956 during the mid-day lunch break or end of day rush. Many factory workers and shoppers are heading up town. Titan TD5 No 54 (AFE 369) and another TD5 of the Corporation fleet, pass by two stationary Bristol K types of the Lincolnshire Road Car fleet. St Marks Street was used for a number of years by the Road Car as a terminal for some of its double deck operated services. At the kerbside is an independently owned Bedford OB.

LINCOLNSHIRE ECHO
Ri/3776.jpg

An Albion articulated tractor hauls a low loader trailer carrying a large drag line excavator manufactured by Ruston Bucyrus at their Beevor Street works. A 1937 Leyland TD5 No 50 (AFE 86) waits whilst the load clears the St Mark's crossroads during rush hour traffic on 5 October 1956.

LINCOLNSHIRE ECHO
Ri/3780.jpg

In September 1957 six new double deckers were placed into service wearing the new bright livery. Nos 75-80 (KVL 679-84) were Leyland Titan PD2/31 with Roe bodies.

These buses had concealed radiators behind louvre style fronts, a feature which quickly earned them the name, "The Tin Fronts".

Route number blinds were fitted on the front and rear. Access to the nearside destination blind was from inside the saloon rather than over the platform.

The saloons had a bright "new look" décor which included pressed steel window trim in place of the traditional dark wood trimmings. These were painted fawn which complemented the white ceilings and the green crocodile leather panelled walls to good effect. Brown linoleum furnished the lower saloon bulkhead and the upper saloon destination box. The seats were upholstered with green leather in the rib style on black tubular steel frames. With the increased seating capacity, large clear route numbers and the clean bright interiors they became very popular with the passengers.

The number of passengers carried had fallen each year since reaching a peak in 1952 and this was an indication that the Department would have to introduce one-man operated vehicles in the near future.

A Leyland Tiger Cub was borrowed for evaluation purposes in February 1955 but it was more than three years before an order was placed with Leyland Motors for seven under-floor engined Tiger Cubs.

These entered service on 1 November 1958. Coachwork was by Roe and of the front entrance, centre exit configuration seating 41 with a high standing capacity of 17. This high number of standing passengers was achieved by the elimination of forward facing seats in the central part of the vehicle. A longitudinal seat for five passengers was fitted on the offside opposite the centre exit and another for three passengers fitted on the nearside, immediately ahead of the doorway.

The idea in theory was that the wide central part of the gangway would facilitate a fast flow of alighting passengers from the centre exit whilst passengers boarded at the front.

In practice the result was very much different, due to the fact that the large number of standing passengers at peak times blocked the exit.

Specifically designed as a one-man operated vehicle, these short wheel base Tiger Cubs, Nos 81-87 (MFE 993-99) were initially crew operated.

Some route changes occurred when Routes 7B Brant Road and 10 Rookery Lane were revised in 1956 to run via Scorer Street. A new service was introduced in 1960 to serve the Ermine Estate West, Route 11. This turned left off the Riseholme Road into the estate. The Burton Road Route 1 had previously been extended circa 1957 to serve the estate on the other side.

The Lincoln engineering firm of Ruston & Hornsby had successfully developed an air cooled diesel engine for marine application and many were in use throughout the world. During 1961 Rustons approached the Transport Department with a view to fitting one of these engines into a bus for experimental use. Guy Arab No 23 had been out of service since 31 October 1959 so it was suggested by the Department that this vehicle could be used for the trial service. The engine was fitted by Ruston engineers at the St Marks depot on 13 June 1961. The bus then re-entered passenger service, on an experimental basis initially. It was very successful from the beginning and the only problems that had to be overcome by Rustons were the excessive vibration and quite colossal noise at high revs (2,200 rpm). To counteract the vibration they insulated the driver's cabin ceiling but this made it very hot to drive in the summertime.

The first new buses to be delivered in the new broad cream livery were the six 1957 Titans. This photograph shows No 80 (KVL 684) at the St Mary's Street terminus on 3 September 1957. The side destination blinds were operated from inside the saloon, a new design feature to prevent head injuries to platform staff leaning out whilst the vehicle was in motion. Twin track route number blinds were fitted at the front and the rear.

LINCOLNSHIRE ECHO
Ri/904B

A nearside view of sister vehicle No 79 (KVL 683) showing the new enclosed tin front bonnet style. The new livery is in striking contrast to that of the two buses in the background. This section of the Central Station car park was on loan from British Railways for boarding and alighting whilst work was being carried out on resurfacing the road on Portland Place by the Grand and Oxford hotels during September 1957.

R MARSHALL COLLECTION

Seven Roe bodied Leyland Tiger Cubs purchased in 1958 were specifically designed for one-man operation. No 87 (MFE 999) stands outside the Crossgates Carriage works of Charles H Roe at Leeds for this photograph just prior to delivery.

CHARLES H ROE/LVVS COLLECTION

Tiger Cub No 87 (MFE 999) heads down Broadgate on a return journey to the City during the 1960s. Today the road is a very busy dual carriageway.

PHOTOBUS

Performance was excellent and this was proven on many occasions on uphill journeys. If a driver got through the traffic lights at Silver Street without being held up, then it was possible to ascend Lindum Hill in top gear with a good load of passengers. The remarkable engine was a credit to both the designers and engineers.

A development of a different kind took place, also during 1961, when the City Council announced the first stage for the setting up of a one-way traffic system in the City centre. The High Street, from St Mary's Street junction to the Stonebow and the upper part of High Street from the Stonebow to Clasketgate, were to become one-way only in the northerly direction. Silver Street would become one-way from Mint Street junction to Broadgate in the easterly direction.

Purchases of new buses reverted to double deckers in June 1961 when two entered service followed by another two in September. Nos 88-91 (RFE 415/16 / SFE 117/20) were variants of the Titan range, being PD2/41 and similar to the earlier batch of Titans purchased in 1957 but fitted with external radiator grilles.

In sharp contrast to the rest of the fleet these buses went into service in a pale green and cream livery similar to that used by Lincoln City Tramways and also on the first buses of Lincoln City Omnibuses. Controversy still remains today as to whether this was a mistake by Charles H Roe coachworks or whether they were ordered in that livery.

The seats were given a clean new look, being covered on the backs with grass green, bubble surface Melamine.

An unusual purchase was the supply of four new AEC Bridgemaster double deck buses in December 1962. Bodywork was also different and built to a low bridge height by Park Royal Coachbuilders of London. Being of integral (no chassis) construction it was possible to achieve normal headroom in the wide central gangways without reverting to a sunken side gangway on the upper deck like that fitted on the TD1s.

These were Lincoln's first 8ft wide buses and the increased width allowed the provision of wider gangways in both the upper and lower saloons.

The absence of grab poles in the upper saloon made it very difficult to walk straight down the gangway when the vehicles were in motion. This was because the Bridgemaster was based on an independent air suspension system on the rear wheels. It was quite a novel experience to see and feel the vehicles bounce when boarding and alighting from the rear platform.

Coil springs were fitted to the front.

Built to an increased length of 30ft, Nos 92-95 (TFE 535-538) were able to accommodate 76 passengers seated, 45 in the upper saloon and 31 in the lower.

During 1963 examples of both the Leyland Atlantean and the Daimler Fleetline rear engined double deckers were borrowed from other operators for evaluation.

The Atlantean was chosen and an order placed with Leyland for the supply of four vehicles for delivery in 1964. Nos 96-99 (WFE 48/49/698/699) came bearing high capacity front entrance bodies built by Roe seating 76 in the form of 43 above 33.

Photograph on previous page.

Guy Arab No 23 (DFE 383) had a chequered service life that employed four different engines. It was originally fitted with a Meadows 6DC, then a Meadows E120 both of which blew up, and then it was tried with a Leyland 8.6 which eventually suffered a cracked block. It was out of service for about a year when Ruston & Hornsby approached LCT during 1961 to use the bus as a test vehicle and fit it with a Ruston air-cooled 6YDA (six cylinder, Y type, diesel, air cooled) engine. It is seen here standing at the foot of Pelham Bridge for an official Ruston & Hornsby photograph to mark its entry into trial service in March 1961. It was withdrawn on 30 November 1967 and presented by Ruston & Hornsby to the Lincolnshire Vintage Vehicle Society and is now part of its renowned collection.

RAY HOOLEY COLLECTION

Three Leyland PD1As were added to the fleet in April 1948. Back then no one would have imagined that such a remarkable photograph would be taken. The swan from the Brayford Pool carefully crosses the High Street in front of No 73 (CVL 771) on 4 January 1961. Note the aluminium winter cover on the radiator grille.

LINCOLNSHIRE ECHO
Ri/3241.jpg

Lincoln chose to revert to exposed radiators for its Titans delivered in 1961. The unusual pale green and cream livery given to these buses suited the neat lines and smooth curves of the Roe body. The first one of the batch No 88 (RFE 415) passes along a busy St Mary's Street during Lincoln Race week of 1962.

PHOTOBUS

A one-way traffic plan for the City centre was announced in the Lincolnshire Echo on 25 August 1961. This photograph taken three days earlier on 22 August accompanied the article to show that very soon, down traffic would not be allowed through the "Bow". The one-way system was introduced on Monday 29 April 1963.

LINCOLNSHIRE ECHO
Ri/3270

Their delivery marked the return of Charles Roe products after the brief association with Park Royal for the supply of the four Bridgemasters.

The new Atlanteans were similarly furnished inside to all the vehicles bought since 1957 with one exception, that being white plastic laminate ceilings replacing the white stove enamelled panels customary to Charles Roe in that period. Beautiful "butter dish" style light globes were fitted in the saloons. These were reminiscent of, yet slightly smaller than, those fitted earlier in both the Tiger Cubs and the Guy Arabs.

A repeat order was placed for four additional Atlanteans and these joined the fleet in August 1965 as Nos 4-7 (AVL 277-280 C).

Around this time the seven Leyland Tiger Cubs, Nos 81-87, began one-man operation for the first time since they were purchased, on four Routes: 5 – St Giles, 9 – Nettleham Road, 7B – Brant Road and 10 – Rookery Lane.

These were the first Lincoln City buses to be one-man operated since the departure of the two Guy B type buses Nos 12/13 over thirty years earlier.

Housing development was taking place on the old Skellingthorpe Aerodrome, south west of the City. The Lincolnshire Road Car Company operated an hourly service from Lincoln St Marks bus station to Skellingthorpe and Jerusalem and so was able to claim the rights to traffic from the new Birchwood Estate. It would have been of immense value to the Corporation if it had been given the licence to operate a route. Revenue was in decline and the Department was incurring heavy losses. To try to prevent further losses it was announced that more routes would have to be one-man operated with the eventual end to all crew operation within a few years.

With that aim in mind the Department ordered four Leyland Titan PD2/37 with Roe 62 seat forward entrance bodies, in 1966. Just why they reverted to front engined vehicles has never been clarified but it is thought to be that they were dissatisfied with the Atlanteans. They had regular periods off the road for somewhat minor problems during their first two years in service.

The new Titans could have been adapted for one-man operation by fitting a swivel driver's seat. This idea was rejected by the trades union members who opposed the idea of one-man operation of double deckers until conditions were revised and rates of pay increased accordingly.

In the autumn of 1966 Leyland launched the Panther, a 36ft long, high capacity, front entrance single decker designed specifically for one-man operation. A demonstration vehicle toured and this came to Lincoln for a week in November. An order was placed for five.

In January 1967 the four forward entrance Titans Nos 8-11 (DVL 356-359E) arrived from Charles Roe. After placing in service eight Atlanteans purchasing Titans again seemed a backward policy. They were however more modern inside than the Atlanteans. Cream patterned laminate was used in place of Rexine for the wall coverings and seat backs. Ceilings were covered with white Melamine like those of the Atlanteans. Fluorescent lights were fitted for the first time and also for the first time on any Lincoln deckers they were unique in having compact spiral staircases, a feature that made possible a higher than normal seating capacity on the top deck for a vehicle of 26ft in length. Their seating capacity was 37 in the upper saloon and 25 in the lower saloon.

The acquisition of four AEC Bridgemasters in 1962 was a most unusual purchase for a fleet predominantly Leyland. It remains controversial whether they may have been part of an order originally placed by Leicester City Transport. The first one of the batch, No 92 (TFE 535), waits on Oxford Street in the City and displays the original broad cream and green livery.

LVVS COLLECTION

The four Bridgemasters were Lincoln's only AEC double deckers. Built by Park Royal Vehicles of London, they were low height vehicles as their name so aptly describes and also to a new with of 8ft. The driver's cabins were fitted with sliding doors. This one, No 95 (TFE 538), was the last one of the batch. It was photographed whilst unloading passengers on St Mary's Street and it wears the livery introduced in August 1963.

GERALD MEAD

The first of a new generation of rear engined double deckers to arrive was No 97. The photograph taken on the Ropewalk in the City shows the low step, front entrance with the staircase directly opposite. Seating capacity was for 76 passengers plus 5 standing. They were fitted with electrically operated, four speed, semi automatic, pneumocyclic gearboxes.

LINCOLNSHIRE ECHO
Ri/2614A

This second photograph shows the very attractive rear bustle that surrounds the vertically mounted Leyland 0.600 engine. The Atlantean was designed for one-man operation but initially this Lincoln batch was crew operated. A rather outdated feature was the external winders on the number tracks. These were realigned to operate from the inside soon after they went into service, no doubt to prevent conductresses marking their uniforms. Both photographs were taken on 11 June 1964, six days before it entered service.

LINCOLNSHIRE ECHO
Ri/2614B

The five Leyland Panthers arrived in May 1967 and the Department planned to add many more to the fleet over the next three years. They decided upon using a clear block of numbers to avoid repeating the rather untidy numbering format of previous rolling stock. The Guys and Leyland PD1s were an example of that.

The first one of the batch No 41 (EVL 549E) had the Leyland 0680 engine and was fitted with green patterned moquette coach seats and luggage racks for dual-purpose bus and coach service. Its capacity was 45.

The other four, Nos 42-45 (EVL 550-553E) had green leather, herringbone style seats with stainless steel grabs on the seat backs. They had a seating capacity of 49 and being solely for bus work were fitted with the Leyland 0600 engine.

In common with the Atlanteans and the four latest Titans they were equipped with bell cords in anticipation of future one-man operation.

Repeat orders were placed for deliveries in 1968 and 1969 becoming Nos 46-49 (GVL 46-49F) and 50-53 (HVL 963-966G).

In 1970 a batch of twelve arrived, Nos 54-65 (KVL 54-65H) bearing similar Roe 49 seat bodies. With the arrival of these buses, eight more routes became one-man operated services from 26 July. These were Routes 1, 3, 6, 8A, 8B, 11, 12, 14. Only six services then remained crew operated, and they were: 2 West Parade, 4 Doddington Road, 7 Hykeham Road, 15 St Georges Hospital, 16 County Hospital, 17 Cemeteries. The works specials continued to be crew operated. The once very popular Sunday Circular Tours were withdrawn in May 1970. These had been in decline for a number of years with the spread of car ownership.

During that year a request for a service came from the residents of the new Boultham area, lying immediately south west of the City centre. This was rejected by the Traffic Commissioners as being unworkable due to the narrowness of Waterloo Street and its double bend a few yards south of the Beevor Street railway crossing.

Mr Herbert Jones, the General Manager retired on 10 June 1970. He was not immediately succeeded in office so his position was covered by Traffic Superintendent Mr John Clayton. In October that year Mr William Dobbie, formerly Deputy General Manager at Aberdeen Corporation Transport, was appointed.

He introduced the "Autofare" system of automatic fare collection in January 1972 on Panther No 65. To operate, the passenger would place the money into a slot above a hopper. This was checked visually by the driver who then pressed the appropriate button on a dashboard panel. The shutter then opened in the hopper allowing the money to drop into the vault below. The ticket was printed and released at the same time from a second box situated on the edge of the cab bulkhead. This system required the exact fare as no change could be given. It was both fast and efficient except when a passenger could not provide the exact fare. The driver would issue a change voucher as a receipt for the passenger to claim his/her money from the offices or the bus inspectors' kiosk in the City.

After taking eight Atlanteans into stock, Lincoln reverted to Titans in January 1967. In anticipation of one-man operation the small window in the centre of the bulkhead was modified on No 10 (DVL 358E) only, to provide a wider aperture to serve passengers. In this early picture it is in original layout.

NIGEL KIRK COLLECTION

This picturesque photograph shows the first Leyland Panther No 41 (EVL 549E) negotiating the beautiful traffic island on Melville Street in May 1967 against the background of the Cathedral. The bus was unique in being the only one of the batch fitted with coach seats and ceiling luggage racks. It is now owned by the author and can be seen at the Lincolnshire Road Transport Museum at North Hykeham, Lincoln.

C V MIDDLETON

A new Leyland Panther, No 43 (EVL 551E), passes beneath the Stonebow on a wet afternoon in May 1967. This was the third bus in a batch of five which were all crew operated until July 1970.

CYRIL COOKE

The Leyland Panthers were the City's first high capacity single deckers designed specifically for one-man operation. This is No 44 (EVL 552E) captured by Peter Grey for the Lincolnshire Echo. It was taken on South Park with the South Common in the background just prior to entering service in May 1967.

PETER GREY

A new circular service, the long awaited North Circular was introduced on 2 January 1972. It offered for the first time, a service linking all the estates in the north of the City, both in clockwise and anticlockwise directions. Route 18A ran clockwise from St Mary's Street via High Street, Yarborough Road, Burton Road, Ermine West, Ermine East, St Giles, Monks Road and St Mary's Street. Route 18B ran anti-clockwise. Leyland Panther No 65 was allocated to the route, being relieved by No 64. Eventually all of the Panthers were equipped with the Autofare system.

The new inner relief road, Wigford Way, opened to traffic on 1 May 1972 linking St Mary's Street with Newland. The High Street, northbound from St Mary's Street to the Stonebow was then closed to traffic and became a pedestrian precinct. The northbound services to the Ermine Estates, St Giles and also services to West Parade, St Georges Hospital and Monks Road all ran via the new road.

In 1972 the Department was inspired to buy Bristol manufacture buses for the first time in its history. Twelve Bristol RE type single deckers with high capacity Alexander coachbuilders 48 seat bodies were ordered for delivery in two batches, The first batch of six arrived between February and April 1973, fitted with the then familiar automatic fare collection equipment to boost the one-man services. A peculiar feature of these six buses was that the large ceiling panels were a different colour and pattern of laminate in each one! The ceiling coving panels though, remained in standard white laminate and fitted with fluorescent lights. The wall panels and seat backs were light green laminate. Window cappings were unpainted aluminium. The seats were covered with dark green vinyl and represented for the first time a move away from the traditional cabbage green crocodile skin pattern leather.

The second batch arrived in October 1973. They only differed from the earlier batch in one detail and that was that they had all been built with standard colour ceiling panels in a shade of grass green. They were Nos 66-71 (RVL 66-71L) and 72-77 (UVL 872-77M).

The first batch became unpopular with many passengers in the summer of 1973 due to the fact that the large panoramic windows did not have any opening vents and they had also been built with only one opening roof vent. The forced ventilation system was inadequate until they were modified. For the first time since 1940 the fleet comprised of mainly single decked vehicles, however things looked set to change. During 1973 an agreement was reached between the management and the Transport and General Workers Union to operate one-man double decked vehicles.

The eight Leyland Atlanteans were duly put onto one-man services with Ultimate ticket boxes but by early 1974 all were fitted with Autofare equipment. With the increase in one-man operated services the Department invited and encouraged conductresses to become drivers. The first two to qualify for the role were Austrian born sisters, Mrs Margaret Barlow and Mrs Freda Littlewood.

A new venture came into being in April 1975 with an attempt to move into the coaching market with the purchase of one new coach.

Westgate Junior School was served by double deckers during the 1950/60s to take children to Ermine Estate West, along the Burton Road. In the 1970s the route was changed to allow single deckers to use Bailgate and Newport Arch. On 11 June 1979 Panther No 62 (KVL 62H) passes beneath the archway, the oldest Roman structure still used by traffic today.

PAUL COOKE

Twelve Bristol RE high capacity single deckers were purchased in 1973 to boost the operation of one-man services. This picture of No 68 (RVL 68L) was taken in its early days in service before the front and rear bumpers were removed. The first six of the batch had inadequate forced ventilation systems until they were modified with opening hatches on their roofs.

PHOTOBUS

An innovative travel scheme to encourage greater use of public transport was launched on 27 March 1979 under the enthusiastic guidance of Mr Peter Sephton in association with Fotomaton Ltd. Photofare provided a photocard and one month of unlimited travel in Lincoln at a prepaid discount price. Bristol RE No 69 (RVL 69L) led the advertising campaign in a striking yellow and cream livery.

CYRIL COOKE

The City bus station has an east side entrance on Melville Street and a west side exit leading onto Norman Street. When it became operational in August 1978, northbound services that used Wigford Way were re-routed via Melville Street, St Swithin's Square and Bank Street. Bristol RE No 77 (UVL 877M) has just departed from the station to the right of the picture for a journey to Ermine Estate on 11 June 1979.

PAUL COOKE

JFW 184N was a Bedford YRT with Caetano bodywork. Licensed as a 46 seater it could be fitted with two tables by the removal of two pairs of seats. It wore a white livery with a leaf green waistband and two narrow green bands on the skirt panels. It was never allotted a fleet number.

In October 1975 five new double deckers arrived, the first to join the fleet for over eight years. Bearing fleet Nos 21-25 and registered (LFE 21-25P) they were Bristol VR type with fully automatic gearboxes. The bodies were built by Eastern Coachworks with a capacity of 77 seats. The layout was 43 seats on the upper deck and 34 on the lower. They were very brightly furnished. The wall panels and seat backs were orange laminate, white and green "crazy" pattern ceilings whilst the cab and platform area were finished in matt black to help prevent reflection for the driver. The seats were covered in green leather with the exception of the rearmost seats on the upper deck. They were made of fibreglass to combat vandalism.

A second batch arrived in 1976, Nos 26-30 (RFE 26-30R) broadly similar to the earlier ones but bearing a different interior colour scheme, they were beautifully furnished. Dark mahogany laminate complemented the seat backs and side panels whist the ceilings were finished in laminate of a small leaf pattern on an ivory background. The seats were upholstered with light brown leather.

Vehicle purchases had now moved in favour of double deckers since the implementation of the Transport Union OMO agreement. This policy was to continue under the guidance of Mr Peter Sephton who succeeded Mr Dobbie as General Manager in January 1978.

Mr Sephton gave his full backing to increase the double decker strength and he also drew up plans to introduce some new routes and extend some existing ones. The most notable of these were Routes 4A and 6A to Birchwood Estate. Operating rights to work the estate were made possible under an agreement reached between Mr Sephton and the Lincolnshire Road Car. In return the Road Car was allowed to pick up passengers on all its routes entering the City. Monks Road Route 3 was extended to include the new Glebe Park estate just off the Wragby Road north of the St Giles estate.

In the City, traffic congestion was becoming an increasing problem particularly on St Mary's Street. To alleviate some of this, a major development got under way in the summer of 1977 with the building of a new City Bus Station on Melville Street. The station is adjacent to a new superstore with a roof top car park and was achieved in a joint venture between the City Council and the Lincoln Co-operative Society. It occupies a site formerly used as a car park and which in earlier years had been home to many different businesses including those of Hall's Brewery, Gilberts garage, The Lincoln Ambulance Service and during the 1950s was a terminal for some services of the Lincolnshire Road Car.

The new bus station opened on 13 August 1978 and the concrete bus shelters on St Mary's Street were demolished immediately to make way for an improved taxi rank.

The Corporation purchased this Caetano bodied Bedford YRT coach in April 1975 for private hire work. It was a 46 seater fitted with a toilet at the rear. The venture was short lived and the vehicle was withdrawn in 1977. In this photograph it is parked on the railway sidings on the Ropewalk. The building in the background is an extension of the old Great Central Warehouse.

PHOTOBUS

As a way of bringing in extra revenue, Lincoln branched out into all over advertising on the buses in March 1978. The first one to appear, Bristol VR No 23 (LFE 23P), in a stunning crimson livery advertised the Lincoln Theatre Royal. Several more vehicles were given all over displays but none was quite as eye catching as the "Theatre bus".

CYRIL COOKE

The 1979 batch of Bristol VRs had East Lancashire Coachbuilders bodywork that was rather box like in appearance. The reason that this coachbuilder was chosen was in part, due to Lincoln's preference for a model that offered forward ascending, safety staircases. No 33 (EFE 33T) is in the livery introduced in 1975. With the exception of the cream front panel, it is a revision of the mid war years livery introduced in 1943.

CYRIL COOKE COLLECTION

Bristol VR No 25 (LFE 25P) stands at the Ermine Estate West terminus on 20 July 1979. It is in a special livery to commemorate 75 years of Corporation transport in Lincoln.

PAUL COOKE

Three new batches of Bristol VRs were added to the fleet during 1979-81 and two batches of second-hand Bristol VRs purchased from Tayside Transport in Dundee during 1980/82. In common with Lincoln's first VRs they all had Gardner engines and fully automatic gearboxes.

The new Bristol buses were Nos 31-34 (EFE 31-34T) with East Lancashire 77 seat bodies. A notable feature of these buses was the special forward ascending staircase requested by Mr Sephton in preference to the rearward ascending type. Brown leather seats were fitted and ivory and fawn laminates used on the sides and ceilings giving a clean, tidy arrangement.

Nos 35-37 (NFW 35-37V) delivered in 1980 were broadly similar to the earlier four but built on a long wheelbase chassis. These had a large seating capacity of 86 plus five standing passengers allowed.

The third batch Nos 38-41 (UFW 38-41W) built to the same specification as Nos 35-37, arrived in 1981. These introduced a revised livery whereby cream became the foremost colour enhanced with two green bands and green roofs.

The eight ex-Tayside Transport VRs were also long wheelbase variants with bodywork built by Alexander to dual doorway configuration. Internally they conformed to the blue and white scheme favoured by the Dundee based operator. They were purchased by Lincoln in 1980/82 and became Nos 87-94 (OSR 187-89/200-03/198R).

Four Leyland Atlanteans were purchased from Leicester City Transport in 1981. They had bodywork built by Eastern Coachworks containing a wide spiral staircase. They were numbered in a somewhat untidy series, 95-97/99 (PBC 101/96/100/99G) due in part to the fact that Lincoln's original No 98 was still in stock having been converted to a driver training vehicle. These buses together with Nos 31-41 and 87-94 ousted the entire stock of twenty four Panthers which inevitably had their service life span shortened following the OMO agreement mentioned earlier.

Production of the Bristol VR chassis came to an end in 1981 and was replaced by Leyland in the form of a semi integral chassis for double deck bodies and marketed under the new name, Olympian.

To continue Mr Sephton's policy of replacing all the high capacity single deckers, successor Mr Mark Beswick ordered one Olympian for evaluation.

East Lancashire Coachbuilders were chosen again and No 42 (DFW 42X) entered service in March 1982 and following a satisfactory service trial three more were put into service in December the same year, Nos 43-45 (KTL 43-45Y).

These buses, in common with the Bristol VR, had fully automatic gearboxes. The 85 seat bodies bore the same colour scheme inside as the previous batch of VRs. This consisted of ivory ceilings and basswood pattern laminate panels. For the first time since the pre-war Guy single deckers Nos 22/23, these Olympians were furnished with Moquette seats throughout, in a bright brown and orange check pattern.

No 45 was unique in being fitted with an electronic destination display.

During 1983 General Manager Mr Mark Beswick suddenly resigned from office for personal reasons. The Chief Executive at City Hall Mr John Thomas, was asked to assume control of the Transport Department until a successor was found with Mr Craig Black as acting Deputy Manager. Mr David Greenwood was duly appointed in the early part of 1984.

Eight second-hand dual doorway Bristol VRs were bought from Tayside Transport in 1980/82. They were modified to single doorway soon after they arrived at Lincoln. Some went into service before conversion including No 89 (OSR 189R), shown here at the Moorland Avenue terminus on Boultham Moor. In November 1980 it received a special cream livery to mark the visit to Lincoln of Her Majesty Queen Elizabeth II.

CYRIL COOKE

The special cream livery applied to No 89 for the Queen's visit was adopted as the standard fleet livery in 1981. The first new buses to arrive in that style were the long wheelbase Bristol VRs. This one is No 40 (UFW 40W) looking resplendent in the spring sunshine at the City bus station during its first week in service on 7 March 1981.

CYRIL COOKE

Four Leyland Atlanteans were purchased from Leicester City Transport in 1981. These were to help with the replacement of the remaining thirteen Leyland Panthers and also to increase the number of double deckers in the fleet. This special photograph of No 97 (PBC 100G) was taken on Long Leys Road by the West Common. It outlines clearly the beautiful rear bustle curves of the Eastern Coachworks body.

CYRIL COOKE

Road works on Dixon Street during November 1982 resulted in services that normally used that street, being diverted along Boultham Park Road and Boultham Avenue. Leyland Olympian No 42 (DFW 42X) with the author driving passes under the Boultham railway bridge. This carried the high level City avoiding line in the south of the City. The line was closed by British Rail in 1985 and the bridge was demolished soon after.

PAUL COOKE

The Birchwood Flyer Route X6 was a limited stop service introduced in 1985. Leyland Olympian No 45 (KTL 45Y) was painted in a special livery to promote the new service which operated on a thirty minute frequency via the inner City relief route, Tritton Road.

DAVID LONGBOTTOM

Part 5 LINCOLN CITY TRANSPORT

A new attractive white livery was introduced in March 1985. The largely white scheme designed by the London consultant Hyphen, was relieved by three bands in varying shades of green and swept up towards the rear. It was continued similarly on the front. The lower green band matched the dark green skirt. The company fleet name became Lincoln City Transport accompanied by a motif of Lincoln Cathedral.

In October 1985 three Leyland Olympians with Gardner 6LX engines were delivered and these became the first new buses bearing the striking white livery. Built by East Lancashire coachbuilders, Nos 46-48 (C46-48 KBE) were 76 seaters with coach seats in grey moquette. The sides and ceilings were also covered in grey fabric. These were bought for long distance operation and private hire but were also used on the City services.

To enable more coach work to be operated in hand with the Olympians, five second-hand AEC Reliances with 53 seat Plaxton Supreme IV coach bodies were purchased and were ex-London Country Bus Services vehicles. These ran for a few months before being allotted a fleet number, eventually becoming Nos 50-54 (211 WVT / UDY 379 / YSV 533 / UXF 718 / XLB 821). One second-hand Olympian was purchased in September 1986, ex-Derby City Transport to replace Lincoln VR No 22 which was damaged by fire in September. The Derby bus had an East Lancs body and became No 49 (A208 ATO).

Lincoln City Transport became a limited company on 26 October 1986 and on that date all bus services throughout Great Britain were subject to deregulation following the Government's policy on transport.

This allowed all companies to tender for routes and services outside the confines of their present operating area. Lincoln City Transport was then able to operate bus services beyond the City boundary for the first time.

A very unusual venture was the purchase of twenty Austin FX4 London Carbodies taxi cabs. These were to be known as the "Lincoln Limos" and began operation on five individual routes at the start of deregulation, 27 October 1986.

Intending passengers would hail the cab in the manner that one would hail an ordinary taxi cab except these travelled on specified routes. These were: Route 21 North Carlton, 22 Hykeham, 23 Birchwood, 24 Brant Road, 25 Glebe Park. Each Limo displayed a destination board in one of five colours appropriate to the route being worked. They also had fleet Nos 1-20 which at the time were a vacant block of bus numbers. Whether or not they were part of the bus fleet or a separate fleet within the Department is controversial. There was no duplication of numbers so it can be assumed they were part of the bus fleet. They were registered D577-596 CRW and painted in the new white City bus livery. Two more were added in 1987 for use by the disabled only and marketed under the name "Dial a Ride". These were registered D390/1 EDU but were not numbered.

Tenders were successful in gaining the right to operate services out of town. The first of these were Routes 51 Branston via Washingborough, 71 Welton, 75 Fiskerton, 61 Carlton le Moorland, 65 Newark.

A new white livery designed by Hyphen, a London based consultant, was introduced in March 1985. The omission of any Lincoln green in the scheme broke with tradition dating back to 1905. The first bus to present the livery to the City was Bristol VR No 32 (EFE 32T).

The success of the first Olympians led to three more being purchased in 1985. Presented in the new white livery Nos 46-48 were the first double decker coaches in the fleet. They were dual purpose and equipped with the new electronic destination displays. Contrary to this one displaying Skellingthorpe, No 48 (C48 KBE) is at the terminus on the Ermine Estate West.

Bearing registration UFX 718, this coach was one of five ex-London Country Bus Services AEC Reliances. The new white, green striped livery suited the Plaxton Supreme IV coach body very well. For some peculiar reason and quite out of character in the Lincoln fleet, these coaches were identified by their registration numbers. After a considerable period in time they were eventually given fleet numbers. UFX 718 became No 53.

RUSSELL KIRK

The Lincoln Limo fleet of twenty Austin FX4 hail and ride cabs was an attempt to give the passengers greater flexibility whilst also confronting competition from other operators. D578 CRW, No 2 and an unidentified one stand amongst the dark, ugly concrete pillars of the City bus station.

KEN PUDSEY

A wide range of day excursions was advertised for summer operation and for this work more coaches were added to the fleet. The first three in April 1987 were No 55 (A839 SYR), a Leyland Royal Tiger with Roe Doyen 44 seat coach body, and two Leyland Tigers Nos 56/57 (FRN 801W / JCW 726W). No 56 had a Plaxton 50 seat coach body whilst No 57 was a Duple Dominant seating 53. A second Duple Dominant IV was purchased, another Leyland Tiger, and this became No 59 (PYE 838Y), a 51 seater. Four more Tigers were taken into stock soon after and became Nos 60-63 (PYE 843/841/842Y / A844 SYR). These had very distinctive 53 seat Laser bodies built by Duple.

In May 1987 a new mini bus was purchased for evaluation on City services. This was No 58 (D751 GBP) a Robin Hood bodied 25 seat Iveco 49.10. To cope with the expansion in services eight second-hand Daimler Fleetline double deckers were purchased. The first four came from the Merseyside Transport fleet and they became the first ever Daimler buses to be owned by Lincoln Corporation.

Their 75 seat bodywork was built by MCW and they were Nos 95-98 (CKC 309/339/341/350L).

The second batch of four was acquired from the Warrington Transport undertaking having originally worked for London Transport. Their 71 seat MCW bodies were built for one-man operation services in London, having front entrances and centre exits. The centre exit was not used on service in Lincoln. Three were fitted with Leyland 0.680 engines, Nos 83/84/86 (MLH 494/484/490L) whilst No 85 (THM 504M) had a Gardner 6LXB unit.

Four Volvo Citybuses with East Lancashire coach style bodies were put into service in April 1988. They were fitted with grey high back seats with matching grey cloth on the sides and ceilings for working long distance services although at times they could be found on City bus services. Peculiarly, they were registered in Northern Ireland as KIB 6474/6527/6620/ 6708, Nos 64-67 in the Lincoln fleet. Electronic destination displays were fitted.

With the introduction of the Volvos into the fleet, more new services were introduced from 31 May 1988 and these included a Lincoln-Newark-Nottingham service, Lincoln-Skegness via Horncastle, Lincoln-Skegness via Mablethorpe and Ingoldmells, and also a service between Skegness and Ingoldmells along Roman Bank.

Eight Leyland National MK2s joined the fleet in June 1988. They were second-hand vehicles originally with Merseyside Transport and were built in 1980 as the standard Leyland product seating 49 with 23 standing passengers allowed. The National was a product of mass production built at Leyland's then new factory near Workington in Cumberland. It consisted of pressed steel components, riveted together to form an integral vehicle. Because of its somewhat utility construction it could be assembled fast, employing a large proportion of semi-skilled workers.

It was very different in comparison to the beautiful pre-war products offered by Leyland Motors, many of them built to customer's own requirements by highly skilled craftsmen/women.

The Lincoln batch were given fleet numbers relating to their registration numbers, Nos 71-75/78-80 (VBG 91-94/84/88-90V).

Leyland Royal Tigers were the pride of many coach operators. Lincoln City Transport No 55 (A839 SYR) was a luxurious 44 seat Roe bodied Doyen, purchased for National Express work and day excursions.

A wide range of day excursions was offered for the summer of 1987 and two Leyland Tigers were bought for this work. No 56 (FRN 801W) was originally a Leyland Demonstrator vehicle. On this occasion it is loading children at Monks Road Primary School.

Robin Hood bodied IVECO 49.10 No 58 (D751 GBP) was purchased for evaluation in May 1987. None was ordered for Lincoln City Transport and it remained the "odd one out". However four were ordered for the Gains-borough town service.

Some National Express contracts were awarded to Lincoln City Transport during 1987 and resulted in four Duple Laser bodied Tigers being purchased. Along with the three earlier Tigers Nos 55-57, they were also originally members of the Grey-Green fleet. All four were operated in the National Express livery. This one is No 60 (PYE 843Y) caught up in traffic on St Mary's Street.

Daimler Fleetlines were trialled in service from time to time yet none was ever purchased new. The expansion of services in 1987 required some extra buses so the opportunity was taken to purchase eight second-hand Daimler Fleetlines. Seen on Nettleham Road in the north of the City is the first one, No 95 (CKC 309L), an ex-Merseyside Transport bus.

CYRIL COOKE

Following the Merseyside Daimler Fleetlines, four ex-London Transport Fleetlines were acquired. Of these, three were fitted with Leyland engines whilst No 85 (THM 504M), also pictured on Nettleham Road, had a Gardner unit.

CYRIL COOKE

The operation of coaches had brought about the reintroduction of manually operated gear boxes to the fleet. An ex-Southend Transport Leyland Titan PD3/6 with Massey 70 seat rear entrance body was purchased for use as a driver training vehicle and for upgrading drivers currently employed. It was also available for private tuition. It became No 99 (CJN 441C) in the fleet.

A Leyland Tiger with Plaxton Paramount 3500 coach body was purchased in 1988 and became No 51 (BAJ 633Y). Two DAF coaches were purchased around the same time and these were numbered 52/53 (C628/31 PAU).

A major development began in early summer 1988 with the establishment of twelve routes operating in Scunthorpe, two circular services in Gainsborough and also services between Scunthorpe-Lincoln and Gainsborough-Lincoln. Nineteen new minibuses were bought for these services. Nos 401-414 (E401-14 BCT) No 425 (E425 XKY) were Renault S56s with Reeve Burgess Beaver 25 seat, forward entrance bodies.

Nos 415-418 (E415-18 BCT) were Robin Hood bodied Iveco Ford 49.10s. These buses, whilst owned by Lincoln City Transport, were not part of the Lincoln City fleet. They were purchased solely for the Scunthorpe and Gainsborough operations. Because they were owned by Lincoln City Transport they merit a place in this text. This new venture, however, was short-lived as a result of strong competition from the Lincolnshire Road Car Company. The Betta Bus routes in Scunthorpe were withdrawn after only six months and all nineteen minibuses were sold to South Yorkshire.

In Lincoln the Limo fleet was in difficulties. They had been useful at the outset to fend off competition but by the end of 1988 they were not paying their way. The entire fleet of twenty cabs was withdrawn in January 1989.

Some of the out of town services to the villages of Saxilby, Skellingthorpe and Waddington were taken off and the eight Leyland National 2s then became surplus to requirements so these too were withdrawn.

A Volvo B10M60 with a Plaxton 49 seat coach body fitted with a toilet was added to the fleet in 1990. Although it was not realised at the time, No 50 (G546 XVL) was to become the final vehicle to be placed into service by Lincoln City Transport in its present form.

In November 1991 Lincoln City Transport was sold to a consortium of employees and Derby City Transport by the Lincoln City Council. The company that originated as a private company in the form of Lincoln Tramways, then became Lincoln Corporation Transport had once again become a private company. Some changes were made in an effort to get it to operate more effectively and efficiently. From 6 January 1992 some routes changed slightly and many had an increased frequency. The automatic fare collection equipment was withdrawn and bus drivers were able to give change when required.

Twelve Dodge minibuses were bought and a new livery comprising three different shades of green with white was introduced. Despite these changes the company experienced financial difficulties and ultimately it was taken over by the Road Car Company in February 1993.

Rationalisation followed immediately with the route network being revised. The fleet was also reorganised and many buses were transferred to other depots within the company. the Road Car livery became universal. From the end of 1997 Lincoln City Transport ceased to operate as a separate legal enterprise and became fully absorbed into the parent company.

Today the name survives and is carried by some of the vehicles that operate the City routes.

Four Volvo Citybuses were placed into service in April 1988. The East Lancashire bodies were fitted with coach seats for private hire contract work but they were also to be found working on the City routes. This is No 66 (KIB 6620) leaving the City bus station for a journey to Birchwood Estate.

PHILIP STEPHENSON

A Leyland National was evaluated in service in the early 1980s but none was purchased new. In 1988 eight second-hand ex-Merseyside, National MK 2s were purchased for recently acquired out of town services. This one is No 78 (VBG 88V) photographed in the City Bus station soon after entering service.

NIGEL KIRK COLLECTION

A new venture for Lincoln City Transport was Stonebow Coaches. This explored the marketing of the coaching side of the company separately from the bus services. It evolved with the purchase of two ex-Barton, Plaxton bodied DAF coaches. Pictured here on a private contract and in the new livery of royal blue, white and cornflower blue is No 53 (C631 PAU).

NIGEL KIRK COLLECTION

Volvo B10M60 No 50 (G546 XVL) was the last vehicle to be placed into service by Lincoln City Transport. It had a high floor Plaxton coach body and is seen here at Leicester on National Express contract work.

CRAIG SCHOFIELD COLLECTION

CITY OF LINCOLN TRAMWAYS FLEET LIST

Fleet No	Truck	Gauge	Motors	Body	Body Details	Seating Capacity	Year New	Year Withdrawn
1	Conaty & Lycett	4' 8½"	2 x 25hp Westinghouse	Brush	Originally open-top*	30/22	1905	1929
2-3	Conaty & Lycett	4' 8½"	2 x 25hp Westinghouse	Brush	Open-top	30/22	1905	1929
4-6	Conaty & Lycett	4' 8½"	2 x 25hp Westinghouse	Brush	Originally open-top*	30/22	1905	1929
7-8	Conaty & Lycett	4' 8½"	2 x 25hp Westinghouse	Brush	Covered top	30/22	1905	1929
	Trailers	4' 8½"	Originally horse-drawn		Covered single deck		1899	1921
9-11	English Electric	4' 8½"	2 x EEC DK30B 40hp	Dick Kerr Preston Standard	Covered top	30/22	1919	1929

*Top covers supplied by Milnes Voss

* No 6 fully enclosed in 1924

LINCOLN CORPORATION FLEET LIST – MOTOR BUSES 1920-1991

Fleet No	Chassis	Body	Registration No	Year New	Years Withdrawn	Seating Capacity
1-3	Dennis CAB	Thompson	FE 3931/32/66	1920	1928	B26R
4-11	Dennis CAB	Thompson	FE 4007/18/30/ 52/64/65/92/93	1921	1928	B26R
12-13	Guy B	Bracebridge	FE 6700/6701	1925	1934	B20F
14-19	Dennis E	Bracebridge	FE 8518-20/ 25-27	1926	1929	B32R
20-21	Dennis E	Bracebridge	FE 8870/71	1927	1929	B32R
22-23	Guy BB	Bracebridge	FE 9806/07	1927	1936	B26D
24	Leyland TD1	Leyland	FE 9755	1927	1951	L24/24RO
25	Leyland PLSC1	Bracebridge	VL 77	1928	1938	B32R
1-2-3/6	Leyland PLSC1	Leyland	VL 300/600/ 01/04	1928	1938 No 2 1940 No 1 1942 Nos 3/6	B30R
26-32	Leyland TD1	Leyland	VL 602/03/05/ 845-48	1928	1948 No 31 1949 Nos 29/32 1950 Nos 26/27/30 1951 No 28	L24/24RO
33-34	Leyland TD1	Leyland	VL 1001/02	1929	1948	L24/24RO
35-37	Leyland PLSC1	Leyland	VL 658-60	1928	1944 Nos 35/36 1945 No 37	B30R
4-5/7-8	Leyland LT1	Applewhite	VL 1262-65	1929	1949 Nos 4/5 1950 No 8 1951 No 7	B33R
14-19	Thornycroft ZB6	Bracebridge	VL 1906-11	1929	1938	B32R
38	Thornycroft BC	Bracebridge	VL 4283	1932	1947	B32R
39	Thornycroft BC	Rainforth	VL 4284	1932	1947	B32R
9-11/20	Leyland PLSC1	LMSR	CH 7915/07/ 05/08	1929	1940	B32R
13/21/40	Thornycroft BC	Vickers	UU 8886/92/90	1929	1940	FB32F
41-44	Leyland TD4	Leyland	VL 8845-48	1936	1952	H30/26R
45-50	Leyland TD5	Leyland	AFE 31-33/84-86	1937	1953 No 48 1957 Nos 45-47/ 49/50	H30/26R
51-60	Leyland TD5	Leyland	AFE 370-72/69/ 73/74//76/75/ 77/78	1938	1954 Nos 53/7/8 1956 No 59 1957 No 55 1958 Nos 51/2/ 4/6/60	H30/26R
61-62	Leyland TD5	Leyland	AVL 409/10	1939	1958	H30/26R
63-64	Leyland TD7	Roe	BFE 418/19	1941	1962	H31/25R
65-66	Guy Arab II	Park Royal	BFE 420/21	1943	1954 No 66 1961 No 65	UH30/26R
10-11	Guy Arab II	Park Royal	BVL 7/8	1943	1962	UH30/26R
12-13	Guy Arab II	Park Royal	BVL 24/52	1944	1964 No 12 1965 No 13	UH30/26R
14-17	Guy Arab II	Park Royal	BVL 162/319/ 320/398	1945	1964 Nos 14-16 1965 No 17	UH30/26R

LINCOLN CORPORATION FLEET LIST CONTINUED

Fleet No	Chassis	Body	Registration No	Year New	Year Withdrawn	Seating Capacity
18-22	Leyland PD1	Roe	BVL 722/24/20/ 21/23	1946	1966 No 18 1968 No 19 1969 Nos 20-22	H31/25R
67-71	Leyland PD1A	Roe	CFE 563-67	1947	1968	H31/25R
72-74	Leyland PD1A	Roe	CVL 770-72	1948	1969 No 74 1970 Nos 72/73	H31/25R
23	Guy Arab III	Guy	DFE 383	1948	1967	H30/26R
1-3	Guy Arab III	Guy	DFE 384-86	1948	1965 No 1 1967 Nos 2/3	H30/26R
35-38	Guy Arab III	Guy	DFE 387/446-48	1948	1965 No 36 1967 Nos 35/ 37/38	H30/26R
39-40	Guy Arab III	Guy	DFE 523/24	1949	1967	H30/26R
5	Leyland Cub	Brush	ABE 347	1937	1954	B20F
24-33	Leyland PD2/10	Roe	EVL 537-46	1951	1970	H31/25R
75-80	Leyland PD2/31	Roe	KVL 679-84	1957	1973	H33/28R
81-87	Leyland PSUC1/1	Roe	MFE 993-99	1958	1973 Nos 81-83/ 87 1976 Nos 84-86	B41D
88-91	Leyland PD2/41	Roe	RFE 415/16 SFE 117/20	1961	1976	H33/28R
92-95	AEC Bridgemaster	Park Royal	TFE 535-38	1962	1975	H45/31R
96-99	Leyland PDR1/1	Roe	WFE 48/9/698/99	1964	1980	H43/33F
4-7	Leyland PDR1/1	Roe	AVL 277/80C	1965	1978 No 7 1980 Nos 4-6	H43/33F
8-11	Leyland PD2/37	Roe	DVL 356-59E	1967	1977	H34/28F
41	Leyland PSUR1/1R	Roe	EVL 549E	1967	1979	DP45F
42-45	Leyland PSUR1/1R	Roe	EVL 550-53E	1967	1978 Nos 42/44/45 1979 No 43	B49F
46-49	Leyland PSUR1/1R	Roe	GVL 81-84F	1968	1975 No 47 1979 Nos 46/48/49	B49F
50-53	Leyland PSUR1A/1R	Roe	HVL 963-66G	1969	1980 No 50 1981 Nos 51-53	B49F
54-65	Leyland PSUR1A/1R	Roe	KVL 54-65H	1970	1980 Nos 56/59 1981 Nos 54/55/ 57/58/60-65	B49F
66-71	Bristol RELL6L	Alexander	RVL 66-71L	1973	1985 No 66 1986 Nos 67-71	B48F
72-77	Bristol RELL6L	Alexander	UVL 872-77M	1973	1982 Nos 72/73/75 1984 No 76 1986 Nos 74/77	B48F
-------	Bedford YRT	Caetano	JFW 184N	1975	1977	C46Ft
21-25	Bristol VRT	ECW	LFE 21-25P	1975	1986 No 22 CT Nos 21/23-25	H43/34F